KT-469-662

Experimental and Nonexperimental Designs in Social Psychology

Abraham S. Ross and Malcolm Grant

Memorial University of Newfoundland

FRANCIS CLOSE HALL
LEARNING CENTRE
UNIVERSITY OF GLOUCESTERSHIRE
Swindon Road
Cheltenham GL50 4AZ
Tel: 01242 532913

WestviewPress
A Division of HarperCollins*Publishers*

Social Psychology Series
John Harvey, Series Editor

Empathy: A Social Psychological Approach, Mark H. Davis

Violence Within the Family: Social Psychological Perspectives,
Sharon D. Herzberger

Social Dilemmas, Samuel S. Komorita and Craig D. Parks

*Self-Presentation: Impression Management
and Interpersonal Behavior*, Mark R. Leary

*Experimental and Nonexperimental Designs in Social
Psychology*, Abraham S. Ross and Malcolm Grant

Intergroup Relations, Walter G. Stephan and Cookie White Stephan

All rights reserved. Printed in the United States of America. No part of this publication may be reproduced or transmitted in any form or by any means, electronic or mechanical, including photocopy, recording, or any information storage and retrieval system, without permission in writing from the publisher.

Copyright © 1994, 1996 by Westview Press, Inc., A Division of HarperCollins Publishers, Inc.

Published in 1996 in the United States of America by Westview Press, Inc., 5500 Central Avenue, Boulder, Colorado 80301-2877, and in the United Kingdom by Westview Press, 12 Hid's Copse Road, Cumnor Hill, Oxford OX2 9JJ

Ross, Abraham S.
    Experimental and nonexperimental designs in social psychology / by Abraham S. Ross, Malcolm Grant.
        p. cm.
    Originally published: Madison, Wis. : Brown & Benchmark Publishers, c1994.
    Includes bibliographical references and index.
    ISBN 0-8133-3006-8 (pbk.)
    1. Social psychology—Research. I. Grant, Malcolm. II. Title.
HM251.R79 1996
302'.072—dc20   96-1277
                                                               CIP

The paper used in this publication meets the requirements of the American National Standard for Permanence of Paper for Printed Library Materials Z39.48-1984.

10   9   8   7   6   5   4   3   2

370215871X

**FRANCIS CLOSE HALL
LEARNING CENTRE**
Swindon Road Cheltenham
Gloucestershire GL50 4AZ
Telephone: 01242 714600

UNIVERSITY OF
GLOUCESTERSHIRE
at Cheltenham and Gloucester

WEEK LOAN

WITHDRAWN

15 OCT 1997   1 0 DEC 1999   6 MAR 2006
3 1 OCT 1997   1 JAN 2000   2 4 MAR 2006
                  1 9 MAY 2000
                  1 3 NOV 2000   8 MAR 2007
15 JAN 1998
                  2 3 MAY 2001   2 7 APR 2007
2 3 APR 1998
                  2 6 FEB 2004   1 8   2009
3 0 APR 1998
- 9 MAR 1999   - 9 MAR 2004   1 8 SEP 2009
1 6 MAR 1999
                  2 6 MAR 2004
2 3 APR 1999   2 4 FEB 2005
1 8 MAY 1999   - 4 MAR 2005
                  1 5 APR 2005

CONTENTS

**SECTION III: ALTERNATIVES TO THE
EXPERIMENTAL DESIGN   72**

**SECTION IV: SURVEYS—MEASURING ATTITUDES
OR OPINIONS OF A POPULATION   94**

SECTION V: ANYTHING NEW? 136

PREFACE

When we do research we are looking for explanations, usually causal explanations—why did this happen, what caused it to happen? If there is a common thread running through this book, it is that researchers should always be searching for alternative explanations. Whenever we read research reports, whether in journals or public media such as newspapers, we should ask the question, could there be *another* reason why this event occurred?

We have divided the book into five sections. In section I we will discuss different types of alternative explanations. In section II we will consider experimental designs and why they are particularly useful in eliminating alternative explanations. In section III we will consider alternatives to experimental designs and where their weaknesses lie in eliminating alternative explanations.

There are times when we do not seek to explain, merely to describe. In section IV we will consider survey methods and how systematic collection of information can minimize alternative explanations. Finally, in section V we will describe recent research directions and discuss a method called meta-analysis for integrating and interpreting the results of many different experiments.

When you finish this book you should be a critical consumer of research. You should search for alternative explanations for the results you read in newspapers, magazines, and scientific journals. You may hear people criticize the results of a study because the researchers did not collect the data systematically or in true experimental fashion. Once you have finished this book you should realize that this criticism is not always legitimate.

There are many different ways of collecting information about the world, some more rigorous than others. Rigor itself is not the final objective; the final objective is eliminating alternative explanations. Although rigorous studies can help in this regard, you should not ignore the results of less rigorous studies. You must search for alternative explanations for the results.

The information in this book is based on our collective research experience and our experience teaching research designs to undergraduate and graduate students. We have tried to write at a level appropriate for upper-level undergraduate students who have taken or are taking a course in social psychology. We have avoided discussing statistics but assume that readers are familiar with basic parametric and nonparametric statistical tests.

We wish to thank our colleagues and students with whom we have, over many years, discussed virtually all of the ideas presented in this book. We are grateful as well to several reviewers, including Robin Anderson, St. Ambrose University; John Fleming, University of Minnesota; Peter Hill, Grove City College; and David Schroeder, University of Arkansas, whose many excellent comments we have tried to incorporate where possible. We extend special thanks to the many people who have tolerated us while we worked. This includes our spouses who didn't complain as our houses fell apart while we wrote on weekends, and Cathryn Button and Ted Hannah who worked constantly to cheer us up. It also includes Bernice St. Croix who ran the department while ASR worked on the book. Finally, I (ASR) thank my mother who read and commented on the earliest version of this book.

SECTION

Causality

Inferences About Causality

The Search for Alternative Explanations

All humans are scientists. We observe nature and the behavior of others. We seek consistencies and the causal rules that help explain these consistencies. Once we understand the rules, we can make predictions. These predictions, if they are accurate, make it easier for us to deal with nature and with the people around us.

Let us consider an example. We see that Michael helps Richard with his assignments, that he lends money to Morris, and that he takes a lost child to the police station. Looking for consistency in his behavior, most observers would agree that his actions are "helpful." However, they might not agree about why Michael has taken these actions. Some might believe that the cause lies outside Michael; for example, Richard may have put pressure on Michael to help him. Others might argue that the cause of Michael's actions is "inside" him; Michael may be a "helpful person."

Some social psychologists study why people choose these alternative explanations for others' behaviors. This area of research is known as *attribution theory*.

Many times people attribute causes for events or for other people's behavior without realizing there are alternative explanations. Someone who believes Michael is a helpful person might not consider the alternative that Richard put pressure on him to help. We may be more likely to overlook alternative explanations when our first explanation fits with our beliefs about the other person.

There are almost always alternative ways of explaining even the most obvious events and behavior. Considering alternative explanations will often prevent hasty and erroneous conclusions. We share the view of Lord, Lepper, and Preston (1984) that many of the judgmental biases to which people are prone can be corrected or lessened by a conscious effort to "consider the opposite."

Like other people, scientists and social psychologists observe, seek consistencies, and infer causal rules to explain them. As you will see, researchers too sometimes overlook alternate explanations for their observations. Much of what we discuss in this book will focus on the search for alternative explanations.

If psychologists and armchair scientists both search for consistencies and causal explanations of behavior, what are the essential differences between them? Two of the most important have to do with how systematically they collect the information and how effectively they can eliminate alternative explanations.

There are several methods of gathering information about thoughts, emotions, behavior, and the variables that may influence them. Some of these methods are more systematic than others. Suppose you are interested in finding out how people will vote in the next election. A less systematic approach might involve asking your friends about their choice of candidates. A more systematic approach might involve administering a questionnaire with highly specific questions to a random sample of a population.

Researchers try to collect information that will tell them whether particular explanations are true or false. Ideally, the information will support one explanation and disconfirm all others. In practice, however, there are usually alternative explanations for any results. Less systematic research methods leave many alternative explanations; more systematic methods leave few. We can classify research designs by their efficiency in eliminating alternative explanations—that is, in terms of how rigorous they are.

As you search for alternative explanations and try to evaluate the evidence for them you should realize that these processes are influenced by your own view of the world. This is true of scientists as well. Mahoney (1977) was interested in the possibility that scientists may allow their own theoretical orientations to bias their evaluations of research reports submitted by other researchers for publication. Typically an article that is submitted for publication is sent by the editor of the journal to three or four well-known researchers in the area for evaluation. The opinions of these reviewers largely determine whether or not the article is accepted for publication.

Mahoney (1977) decided to use as subjects in his experiment the 75 referees listed by the *Journal of Applied Behavior Analysis* for the year 1974. This journal publishes articles "advocating the refinement and expansion of applied behavioristic psychology" (Mahoney, 1977, p. 164) and the theoretical perspective of the reviewers was assumed by Mahoney to be clearly in this direction.

To each of the reviewers Mahoney sent a manuscript which he told them was being considered for inclusion in a volume titled "Current Issues in Behavior Modification." In addition to responding to some open-ended questions, each reviewer was asked to evaluate the manuscript in terms of the relevance of its topic, its methodology, the presentation and discussion of the data, and its scientific contribution. Finally, each reviewer was asked to make a recommendation concerning the manuscript: accept, accept with minor revisions, accept with major revisions, or reject.

The manuscript that Mahoney fabricated for the purposes of his experiment dealt with the effects of reinforcement on intrinsic motivation. The traditional behavioristic position on this question is that when people are reinforced for working on a task, their motivation increases. Other psychologists have challenged this idea and have argued that extrinsic reinforcement can sometimes result in diminished intrinsic motivation. The fictitious manuscript which Mahoney devised described an experiment with children which attempted to test the validity of these two competing points of view.

Mahoney created five versions of the manuscript and each reviewer received one of these versions to evaluate. In one version of the manuscript, the results described were positive in the sense that they supported the behavioristic prediction of increased motivation following reinforcement. (Remember that this is the theoretical orientation presumably held by the reviewers.)

A second version of the manuscript described negative results which refuted the behavioristic prediction. This was done in part simply by reversing the identification labels on the lines of a graph in the first version. A third and fourth version of the manuscript contained mixed results which could be interpreted as either supporting or refuting the behavioristic prediction. In the third version, the mixed results were followed by a "positive" discussion in which the author concluded that the results supported the behavioristic point of view. In the fourth version, the conclusion in the discussion was that the results refuted the behavioristic point of view.

Apart from these variations all versions of the manuscript were identical in terms of the procedural details, bibliography, etc. Reviewers rated the study with negative results as having the least relevance, the weakest method, the weakest data, and as making a relatively minor contribution. The studies with negative results or mixed results were most likely to be rejected.

The reviewers were more likely to reject the study with results that didn't agree with their theories. Even though the methods were the same in all versions, the reviewers rated the method in the rejected study as weaker. Mahoney's results indicate a considerable degree of bias on the part of the scientist-reviewers in the direction of their own theoretical perspective.

Students and other nonscientists often hold the view that science is a purely objective, value-free enterprise. According to this view, the design of scientific experiments is dictated by the research hypothesis and the conclusions that are drawn are dictated by the results. Moreover, scientists may be thought to be less susceptible than are other people to preconceptions and biases. The results of the Mahoney experiment that we have just described clearly challenge this view. Scientists, like other people, are vulnerable to bias and hasty judgments and, again like other people, they can benefit from being reminded of it. An awareness of the possibility of alternative interpretations can be an enormous benefit to researchers both in the design and interpretation phases of their work.

Evidence That X Causes Y

In everyday conversations we often use the concept of causality. We ask, "What caused you to do that?" Or we may ask a friend, "Why did Sarah tell Charles that I liked him?" In this case "why" means, what *caused* Sarah to tell Charles. We search for causes or explanations of events and behavior occurring in the world around us, and in searching for an explanation, we may think of several possible causes. Perhaps Sarah behaved in a certain way because she is angry with me. Maybe she did it because she thinks it would help our relationship. When scientists search for such possible causes they think of them as **causal hypotheses.**

A causal hypothesis often takes the form, "If X then Y." "If I comment on John's weight, then he will become angry." "If I help Jane with her term paper, then she will help me with mine." People find it comparatively easy to generate these kinds of causal hypotheses. Such hypotheses may stem from a need to explain what has already happened and predict what is about to happen.

If you read mysteries you know that detectives often have hypotheses, or hunches about "who done it." Their problems occur when they try to find evidence to support their hypotheses. For the scientist, like the detective, it may be difficult to collect evidence that a particular hypothesis is correct. The fictional detective has one advantage over a scientist. When she uncovers all of the evidence she can confront the villain and know that she was right.

As scientists we can never *prove,* logically, that any hypothesis is correct. No matter how many instances of an event we see, we cannot be sure that it will recur. It is logically impossible to prove that the sun will rise tomorrow. All scientists can do is gather evidence to support or disconfirm an hypothesis. Let us consider the kinds of evidence that are necessary.

There are, in general terms, three kinds of evidence that are useful for supporting or disconfirming an hypothesis:

1. evidence that X and Y occur together
2. evidence that X precedes Y and,
3. evidence that alternative explanations for our results are unlikely.

Evidence That X and Y Occur Together

The first evidence we need is that X and Y occur close together in time. In general, the closer X and Y are in time, the greater the likelihood there is a causal connection between them. When X and Y can occur together in varying degrees, we look for evidence that changes in X occur together with changes in Y. For instance, as we step down on the gas pedal in a car, the car goes faster. In some cases, the association may be of a negative kind; increases in X are associated with decreases in Y. The more novocaine the dentist injects, the less pain the patient feels. We call the variation of X and Y together **concomitant variation.**

A variety of statistical tests are available for detecting concomitant variation between variables and assessing the strength of the association. In fact, of the three kinds of evidence, this is the only one we can assess statistically. We can establish that X precedes Y and eliminate alternative explanations only with systematic data collection and good experimental designs.

Evidence That X Precedes Y

Evidence of concomitant variation alone does not warrant the conclusion that X is causing Y. We need to be sure that X precedes Y. Although this is an obvious point, it is overlooked surprisingly often. Consider the following example. Gerbner et al. (1976) reported that people who watch a lot of television, compared to those who watch less, are more likely to fear that they will be involved in some kind of violence in the near future. Although Gerbner et al. (1976) considered many alternative explanations for their finding, they eventually concluded that watching a lot of television causes people to fear violent crime.

Gerbner and colleagues (1976) did not consider the possibility that heavy television viewing was a consequence rather than a cause of people's fear of crime. Citizens who fear crime may be less likely to venture out of their homes, particularly at night. Since they do not go out, they may spend more time watching television.

Establishing the correct time order will sometimes involve considering additional variables and gathering new data. Doob and Macdonald (1979), for example, discovered that people who lived in areas of the city with a high crime rate, compared to those in areas with a low crime rate, were more likely to fear crime and more likely to be frequent viewers of television. In neither the high nor the low crime areas, however, did the researchers find any relationship between fear of crime and television viewing. Researchers need to be alert to the possibility that different causal sequences may underlie the data they are attempting to explain.

Evidence That Alternative Explanations Are Unlikely

Once we have determined there is concomitant variation and that X indeed precedes Y, we must try to reduce the number of alternative explanations for the X–Y relationship. Usually, alternative explanations will take the following form: "It is not really X that is causing Y but rather another variable, Z." Z is associated with both X and Y.

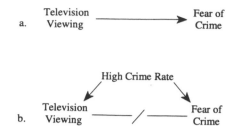

FIGURE 1.1
Alternative explanations—possible interpretations of the relationship between television viewing and fear of crime.

Gerbner et al. (1976) concluded that watching television led to fear of crime (figure 1.1a). Doob and Macdonald found that television viewing did not cause people to fear crime. Rather, the high rate of crime in their neighborhoods led people to spend more time indoors and watch more television (figure 1.1b).

One way to eliminate this alternative explanation is to demonstrate that Y is unlikely in the absence of X. In experimental research, this is the reason for including one or more control conditions. In the example of nonexperimental research considered above, we would look for evidence that people who rarely watch television are less likely to fear crime, regardless of how much crime is actually going on in their respective neighborhoods. Doob and Macdonald (1979) showed this was a viable alternative explanation for the results of the study by Gerbner and colleagues (1976).

The elimination of alternative explanations *after* we complete a study can be frustrating. It is much easier to reduce the number of possible alternative explanations from the beginning. We can do this through careful attention to the principles of good research design.

Internal Validity

Some research designs are more effective than others at minimizing alternative explanations for their results. In this connection, Campbell and Stanley (1963) introduced the concept of the **internal validity** of research designs. Internal validity has to do with the effectiveness of an experimental design to minimize alternative explanations for obtained results. Experiments that have high internal validity do not allow many alternative explanations. Threats to internal validity occur when the researcher allows events other than the ones of interest to vary in an uncontrolled fashion. Let us imagine a city council member who, while walking to work, notices litter on the streets. The council member persuades the city government to start a "Clean Streets" advertising campaign. A few weeks later the council asks the city engineer to check on street litter to see if the campaign has been effective. The engineer reports seeing very little litter on the streets.

Should the city council conclude that the campaign has been effective? Besides the advertising campaign, there are many other factors that could have caused the different observations of the council member and the city engineer. The council member may have observed the streets in the spring. The litter that accumulated during the winter may not have been cleared away. The engineer may have observed the streets in the summer, after city work crews had been busy. Campbell and Stanley (1963) referred to this threat to internal validity as **history.** Events associated with the mere passage of time or events occurring outside the experiment may produce an effect that is mistakenly attributed to the independent variable.

Another possibility is that the differences between the observations of the council member and the engineer reflect differences in the observers rather than differences in what they observed. Perhaps they each have different definitions of "litter." The council member might define anything on the sidewalk impeding a pedestrian as litter, even children's toys. The engineer, on the other hand, might define only loose paper, garbage, etc. as litter. Campbell and Stanley referred to this kind of threat to internal validity as **instrumentation.** What appears to be the effect of an independent variable may be nothing more than the effect of a change in measuring instruments. (In the example we can think of the council member and the engineer as the measuring instruments.)

History and instrumentation are only two of the threats to internal validity that Campbell and Stanley (1963) discussed. We will introduce and discuss other threats to internal validity when we deal with particular kinds of research designs.

External Validity

Campbell and Stanley (1963) also introduced the concept of the **external validity** of a research design. External validity refers to the generalizability of the results. A study has external validity if its results apply to populations and settings other than those actually studied. For instance, would the effect of the Clean Streets campaign be the same in cities other than the one studied? If so, the original study has external validity.

Usually a study must have internal validity in order to have external validity. For example, what if the apparent reduction in litter was the result of the differences between the city council member and the city engineer? In this case, the campaign would not be likely to have the same impact in another city because different people would assess the amount of litter.

Suppose people living in the city where the council conducted the Clean Streets campaign were aware that they were part of a special project to clean up the city. Because of this, they made a special effort to keep the streets clean. It is not uncommon for people's behavior to change when they know they are being studied. If this were the case, we could only generalize the results to situations where people knew they were being studied. If the council in another city mounted the same kind of advertising campaign but people were unaware that they were part of a study, the campaign might have little effect.

In the next chapter we will consider the internal and external validity of a variety of experimental research designs. However, before we do that we will consider some of the ethical problems faced by social psychological researchers.

Ethical Problems

By virtue of the material they study and the methods they use, social psychologists encounter ethical problems not faced by researchers in other areas. In this section we will consider some of the ethical problems that researchers in social psychology encounter as well as some of the safeguards that are available to them.

Stress

Although the great majority of research studies in social psychology involve little if any stress for the participants, there are exceptions. For example, some kinds of experimental manipulations may make people feel fearful (e.g., Schachter's 1959 study of affiliation), guilty (e.g., Milgram's 1963 study of obedience), or apprehensive about how they are being evaluated (e.g., Schmitt et al., 1986). In some cases, such as the examples just cited, the stress is an integral part of the research hypothesis that is being tested. In other cases, the stress is incidental to the main purpose of the research. Although some people might argue that no amount of stress can be justified, a more common position is that some stress to participants is acceptable if the research can be accomplished in no other way.

But how should we evaluate stress and what levels are acceptable? There are no absolute answers to these questions but there are some guidelines that can be helpful. First, we can compare the stress engendered by the research procedures with the stress that the participants might be expected to encounter in their everyday lives. If the stress for the subjects is similar, both qualitatively and quantitatively, to the stress to which they are accustomed, then there may be little reason for concern. Second, the duration of the stress should be taken into account. Ideally, the period of stress should be brief and terminated with a complete debriefing before the subject leaves. A final guideline in deciding whether a given amount of stress is justifiable involves judgments about the importance of the research and whether or not the researcher's purposes could be accomplished in any other way. The principle here is a simple one— stress-inducing procedures should be used only as a last resort.

Invasion of Privacy

All research in social psychology involves extracting information from people, information about their attitudes and beliefs, their perceptions of social situations, and their interactions with other people. A problem arises if the information is personal in nature or if, for some other reason, the participant is unwilling to provide it. The person can, of course, decline to participate or to answer particular questions. In some research, however, people may be studied without their awareness and in these cases the problem of invasion of privacy can be especially serious. Even if people know they are being studied, they may not know the full implications of the information they are providing. This is often the case, for example, with personality and other self-report questionnaires. When planning a research project, it is sometimes useful to consider whether any potential subjects, with full knowledge of the information they will provide and the interpretations to be placed on it, would decline to participate.

Deception

Occasionally, social psychologists find it necessary to deceive their subjects about one or more aspects of the research project. Sometimes the deception is needed in order to manipulate the independent variable (for example, telling subjects that they will receive electric shocks in order to make them fearful). Other times, deception may be used to divert subjects' attention from the main purpose of the study in the hope that their behavior will be more natural.

Several psychologists (e.g., Baumrind, 1985; Kelman, 1967) have expressed concern about the ethics of deception. They feel that to deceive a subject is to treat that subject like an object rather than a human being. In addition, deception may damage a subject's self-concept and leave him or her with an unfavorable view of psychology and its practitioners. Finally, when social psychologists resort to deception, they may damage their own self-concepts and their view of their profession.

Kelman (1967) argued that deception in social psychological research could lead subjects to distrust all psychological researchers. There are many anecdotes about people not helping in a real emergency because they thought it was part of an experiment. One of the authors was investigating bystander intervention in emergencies. His research assistant's car had a flat tire while he was on his way to work. A number of people came in to the author's office that morning, remarked on observing the research assistant on the side of the road, and explained that they hadn't helped because they assumed it was part of his research. Similarly, experimenters who conduct research in cognitive psychology, where deception is rare, sometimes report that subjects are dissatisfied with the explanations they are given after an experiment. The subjects are reported to say things like, "Come on, you can tell me what it's *really* about."

Anecdotal evidence like this suggests that subjects are becoming less trustful of researchers. To see if this is true, Sharpe, Adair, and Roese (1992) compared students' attitudes towards psychological research in December of 1970, in October of 1989, and again in March of 1990. Students in 1970 and 1989 had not participated in any psychological experiments. Subjects in 1990 had taken part in an average of 3.5 experiments.

There were no differences between the students' attitudes in 1970 and 1989. Thus, students who had not been in experiments had not become more negative towards psychological research in the two decades. Sharpe, Adair, and Roese found that students tested in March 1990 had more negative attitudes toward psychological research than students in the other two groups—although these negative attitudes did not appear to be focused on the deceptive nature of the research.

However, these results *do* suggest that students are more negative towards psychological experiments after they have participated in one. There is also an alternative explanation—we do not know what else occurred between October, 1989 and March, 1990. The difference between the groups could be due to the experience of being a subject, but it could also be due to other events. Perhaps in March students were near final examinations, or maybe they were getting tired of the winter weather, and were more negative in general.

Both the American and Canadian Psychological Associations (APA and CPA) have strict ethical guidelines governing the use of deception in research. These guidelines (see appendix A) state that researchers who use deception in an experiment must explain the deception to the subject after the experiment. The experimenter should also insure that the subject fully understands the purpose of the experiment and the deception. Unfortunately, it appears that the impact of some kinds of deceptions cannot be fully eliminated afterwards (Walster, et al., 1967).

Despite concerns about deception, its use in social psychology does not appear to be lessening (Christensen, 1988). In 1985 the frequency of deception in social psychological research had not declined from the early 1970's (Adair, Dushenko, & Lindsay, 1985).

Ethical Safeguards

Informed Consent

The fully informed consent of research subjects is considered by many to be the major ethical safeguard in any research project. When we examine informed consent closely, however, we find that it may be disconcertingly rare in social psychological research.

Consider first the "informed" part. For a subject, being fully informed would mean having all the information about the study that the investigator has. In practice this is rarely the case. In some cases information may be withheld because of its complexity. More often, however, full information about a social psychology study is withheld from potential research participants because of the fear that such information might influence the behavior being studied. Imagine a researcher interested in the effect of physical attractiveness on dating. In one situation she tells subjects that the study is being conducted to see if they preferred to date people who are more attractive than they are or people less attractive than they are. In the other she does not tell them the point of the study. It is likely that subjects' behavior in the two conditions would be quite different. And even if the behavior were the same, it would certainly have occurred for different reasons. Thus, in many cases information is deliberately withheld from subjects.

In experiments where there is deception the whole concept of informed consent is, of course, negated. Under these circumstances, especially serious ethical and legal problems may arise if the study involves any degree of stress for the participants. We may ask, for example, would subjects have agreed to participate had they known at the outset exactly what would be involved? Unless this question can be answered confidently in the affirmative, we may be on very shaky grounds from an ethical and legal standpoint (but see Christensen, 1988, for a defense of deception techniques).

Some researchers have suggested that one way to deal with the problem of informed consent may be to tell all subjects at the beginning that some aspects of the study may not be as they initially appear, that stress may be involved, and that it will be necessary to withhold a complete explanation of the study until all the data have been gathered. Subjects who volunteer under these conditions are, in effect, consenting to not being fully informed. Unfortunately, the legal status of such an agreement is unclear and in addition, many social psychologists would be concerned about the naturalness of a subject's behavior after such an agreement was struck.

What about the "consent" part of informed consent? Consent, of course, means voluntary consent. The subject must feel free to refuse to participate and free to refuse to continue participating at any time during the study. Refusing to participate may, however, be very difficult if large inducements are offered or veiled threats are involved—as may be the case whenever the person doing the research is in a position of power or authority over the potential subject. People may simply feel that they cannot afford to refuse. As examples, consider students who are invited to "volunteer" for a professor's research project or prison inmates who are encouraged to take part in a project and are told that participation will be viewed favorably by the parole board. Certainly compensation for subjects is desirable and may even lessen ethical concerns arising from the induction of stress. At some point, however, compensation can turn into coercion and the notion of voluntary consent may be negated.

Anonymity and Confidentiality

Ethical concerns about invasion of privacy can sometimes be addressed by simple measures to maintain the confidentiality of subjects' responses. Such measures should be implemented routinely and assurances given to subjects in this regard. In many cases it is possible to go further and maintain not just confidentiality but anonymity as well. In these cases, once the data are collected, even the researcher may be unable to associate particular responses with particular individuals.

Debriefing of Subjects

Whether or not subjects have been paid for their participation, most researchers feel obligated to take some time at the end of the research session to explain the procedures and answer any questions (called **debriefing**). At this time, any lingering effects of a stressful manipulation can be detected and removed. Also, the reasons for any deception can be explained and assurances given about measures to protect the anonymity or confidentiality of the information the subject has provided.

Review by an Independent Ethics Committee

In virtually all colleges and universities in North America, research proposals that involve the testing of human subjects are scrutinized by ethics review committees. The people on these committees have no direct connection with the research and can thus provide an independent assessment of whether or not ethical standards are met. Approval of an ethics committee is required before a research project may be carried out. This kind of review procedure offers protection not just for the research participant but for the researcher as well who may inadvertently overlook some ethical problem or neglect to take some precaution.

Summary

We all look for reasons why things happen in the world around us. Often we infer causes without questioning our conclusions. However, scientists look for evidence to support or disconfirm their causal hypotheses. There are three kinds of evidence that are useful for this purpose: X and Y occur together (concomitant variation); X precedes Y (time order); and alternative explanations for the relationship between X and Y are unlikely.

Some research designs are more effective than others at minimizing alternative explanations for their results. Internal validity has to do with the effectiveness of a research design at minimizing alternative explanations. We also want to be able to generalize the results of our research design to other situations, people, and times. External validity has to do with the effectiveness of a research design at allowing us to generalize the results.

By virtue of the material they study and the methods they use, social psychologists encounter ethical problems not faced by researchers in other areas. The problems include the stress of being in an experiment, invasion of privacy, and the use of deception. Ethical safeguards have been introduced to protect subjects. Informed consent, usually considered a safeguard, is difficult to obtain in most social psychological research. Sometimes ethical concerns, such as invasion of privacy, can be addressed by maintaining anonymity and confidentiality. Subjects should be debriefed after being in an experiment. Finally, in virtually all colleges and universities in North America, research proposals that involve the testing of human subjects are scrutinized by ethics review committees.

In the next chapter we will go into more detail about internal and external validity. We will discuss threats to internal and external validity and how specific research designs deal with these threats.

Experimental Research

CHAPTER

Experimental Designs

Imagine a naive observer who sees his children (five and eight years old) fight after watching a violent program on television. He suspects that exposure to television violence leads to aggressive behavior and wishes to gather some research evidence. However, because he is not sophisticated, his research designs will not be rigorous (at least not in our examples).

For his first study, our naive observer wants to find out if other children behave aggressively in similar situations. The observer is sophisticated enough to know that he must design a systematic method of recording and scoring the aggressiveness of the children's behavior. With this in mind, he visits homes of his friends who have children between five and eight years old. He observes the children as they watch violent cartoons on afternoon television programs. After the program, he records each child's behavior, taking care to include only those children who watched the entire program.

In discussing research designs we will use the abbreviations O and X. The symbol O will indicate an observation. This is a point in the research process where we record data. The symbol X will indicate the occurrence of some event that we expect might influence observations that follow it. The researcher may manipulate the event or it may be outside the researcher's control.

Using these symbols we can describe this study as an X–O design. In this case, X is the television program viewed by the children and O is the behavior recorded afterward. The observer finds results that appear clear-cut; the children behave aggressively after watching the program.

What factors threaten the internal validity of the X–O design? In other words, what alternative explanations are there for the observer's results? The most obvious one is that these were aggressive children. They may have been aggressive before watching the program and they might have behaved as aggressively had they not watched the program. Perhaps aggressive children choose to watch violent cartoons. The researcher has no information that would help rule out this possibility. The threat to the internal validity caused by not knowing preexisting behaviors is called **selectivity** because it refers to the possibility that the subjects were selected for the conditions in some biased fashion. For instance, if they chose to watch the program they might be considered self-selected. As you might suspect, there are other threats to the internal validity of this kind of design. We will discuss them when we discuss two more complicated research designs.

To examine the possibility that children play aggressively with or without the influence of television violence, the researcher designs a second study. This time he chooses an O–X–O design; he observes children before and after they watch television. Let us assume that the children do not behave aggressively before watching the program. After the program, however, their behavior is much the same as that observed in the first study. The researcher has reduced the likelihood of one threat to internal validity—selectivity. He knows that the children's aggressive behavior was not aggressive before the program began. Aggressive children do not seem to be likely to choose (or self-select) to watch the program. He has eliminated one threat but several others remain.

One of the remaining threats to internal validity is history. There may well have been other events besides the television program that caused the change in the children's behavior between the first observation, O_1 and the second observation, O_2. Such extraneous events may be external to the individuals the researcher is observing. For instance, there may be many advertisements in the television program, contributing to impatience on the part of the viewers. Or the extraneous events may be internal. For instance, the children may become increasingly hungry as the afternoon progresses, leading to increased aggressiveness.

The threat to internal validity caused by changes or events within the people being observed is called **maturation.** In a literal sense, of course, this term would be more appropriate when longer periods are involved. For example, if we observed children's behavior at the beginning of the school year and again at the end, we would likely find that some changes had occurred. Some of these changes might be due to what the children had learned in school, but others might be due to physical and emotional maturation. We will use this term to describe any change internal to the individual, no matter what the time span.

The distinction between historical and maturational threats to internal validity is not always clear and, in fact, is not that important. The reason for considering threats is not to develop a precise taxonomy or system of classification. The objective is to heighten your awareness of potential problems in research design and to point toward possible solutions.

There are additional threats to the validity of the O–X–O design. One of these is **testing.** The act of observing and measuring behavior can sometimes cause it to change. For example, if we measure people's attitudes toward abortion on two occasions, their responses on the first occasion might influence their responses on the second; the respondents might try to be consistent. In the television example it is possible that the children's knowledge that they are being watched will affect their behavior. (They may try to entertain the observer.)

One last threat we will consider here is that of **instrumentation.** As we said when we considered the Clean Street Campaign in the previous chapter, instrumentation is a threat when the measuring instrument (or observer) changes between O_1 and O_2. Differences in the questionnaire the researcher uses or in the observers who administer it from the first time to the second time leave the results open to the threat of instrumentation. In the present case—involving television and aggression—the observer might be bored by the time of the second measurement. Or, after watching the cartoon with the children, the observer might be more sensitive to aggressive behavior in others.

After completing the initial *X–O* study, the researcher was faced with two questions:

1. How aggressive were the children before they watched the television program?
2. How aggressive would they have been if they had not watched the program?

The *O–X–O* design helped to shed some light on the first of these questions but did not help with the second one. To obtain information about the second question, the researcher could conduct an *X–O* study and include a control group. In the original *X–O* design the researcher observed children who watched an aggressive television program. For this new design, *X–O* with control group, he would again observe children who watched an aggressive television program. However, he would also observe the behavior of children who spent the same time watching a nonviolent program—the control group. He could then compare the aggressiveness of the children in the two groups.

Assume that the researcher carries out such a study and that the results are clear. Children who watch the violent program behave more aggressively afterward than do children who watch the nonviolent program. Now what alternative explanations have we eliminated? History is no longer a threat because any extraneous events would presumably affect children in both the experimental and control groups. Similarly, we can rule out maturation, testing, and instrumentation. However, there is still the problem of selection. Because the children chose the program they wanted to watch, it is possible that the more aggressive children ended up watching the violent program.

Mortality is the last alternative explanation that we will consider. Mortality occurs when people drop out of a study before it is finished. For instance, in a survey, some subjects may move out of the sampling area between the first and second questionnaire. In the aggression–television study, mortality would occur if some children stopped watching either the violent or the nonviolent television program before it was over. It is difficult to interpret the results of a study without knowing the characteristics of those subjects who were lost.

Even when mortality appears to be equal in different conditions there may be a problem. In our example, a child might stop watching a program because it seems boring. Less aggressive children might find the violent cartoon boring while more aggressive children might find the nonviolent cartoon boring. As a result, the children who continued to watch the violent cartoon might be those who were more aggressive and those who continued to watch the nonviolent program might be those who were less aggressive.

Although there are many threats to the first (X–O) and the third (X–O–Control) designs, there are times when they may be the only designs available. For instance, a researcher interested in post-traumatic stress syndrome might want to determine how people cope with airplane crashes, earthquakes, tornadoes, etc. These are events that usually occur without warning. The researcher could use an X–O design and study the people after the event. Or, if there is a comparable group the researcher can use the X–O–Control design. We will have more to say about this kind of situation when we consider nonexperimental designs.

Experimental Designs

Earlier, we said that to establish causality, a researcher must demonstrate, "If X then Y" and "If not X then not Y." The experimental method is the most powerful method for doing this. In an experiment we manipulate X, the **independent variable,** and observe Y, the **dependent variable.**

In a study of the effects of television on aggression, the experimenter might manipulate the type of program watched (the independent variable). The effect of the manipulation on the children's later behavior (the dependent variable) is recorded. The manipulation of the independent variable distinguishes a true experimental design from preexperimental designs (discussed earlier), and from nonexperimental designs (to be discussed in the next chapter).

When social psychologists talk about "manipulating" the independent variable, they usually mean that one group of subjects will be exposed to one set of conditions, X_1, and another group to a different set of conditions, X_2. For simplicity, we will limit our discussion to X_1 and X_2. Although there is no theoretical limit to the number of X's that we may consider, logistical and statistical interpretations can create limitations.

As researchers design their experiments, conditions X_1 and X_2 will differ on some independent variable (X). X_1 may involve the presence and X_2 the absence of some treatment. In this case, the **experimental group** is made up of subjects who experience the treatment and the **control group** is made up of subjects who do not experience the treatment.

Ideally, the experimental and control groups should be identical except for the experimental treatment. Any other difference between the conditions leaves room for an alternative explanation for the results.

Gantner and Taylor (1988) used a treatment–no-treatment design to investigate the influence of a tranquillizer (diazepam) on aggressive behavior. Subjects randomly assigned to the treatment condition were given a 10 mg capsule of diazepam. Subjects randomly assigned to the no-treatment condition were given a capsule that looked identical but contained no drug. The dependent measure concerned the subjects' level of aggression when given the opportunity to inflict an electric shock on a fellow subject. (Of course, no one was ever shocked.)

The Gantner-Taylor study found that subjects who had been given the drug inflicted higher levels of electric shocks on a fellow subject. The drug increased aggressive behavior. The researchers speculated that its tranquillizing effect made the subjects less concerned about the aversive consequences of their behavior.

Another variation on the treatment–no-treatment design is the classic experiment by Schachter (1959). Schachter investigated the relationship between anxiety and affiliation by manipulating whether subjects expected severe or mild electric shocks; this was the independent variable. He then asked subjects whether they wanted to wait alone or with other subjects while the experimenter set up the shock apparatus; this affiliative choice was the dependent variable. Schachter wanted to find out if anxiety (about the shocks) made subjects want to affiliate with other subjects. He found that people who anticipated severe shocks, compared to those who anticipated mild shocks, expressed a stronger preference for waiting with others. In this experiment, Schachter exposed his subjects to one of two different levels of the independent variable (rather than giving a treatment to one group and no treatment to another). This is a common procedure in social psychological experiments.

When we include only two levels of the independent variable in an experiment, as Schachter did, we can obtain a limited amount of information about the relationship between the independent and dependent variables. If we graphed Schachter's results by plotting anxiety on the x–axis and affiliative tendency on the y–axis, there would be only two points on the graph. The line connecting the points would, of course, be a straight one.

What if Schachter had included a third condition in his experiment and told people in this condition that they would receive

of moderate intensity? Would the point representing the af-
tendencies of people in this group fall on the straight line
on the other two points? It might, but there are many other
bilities. In general, it is a good idea to examine the dependent
ble at several different levels of the independent variable. Only
his way can the researcher draw firm conclusions about the na-
of the causal relationship in question.

Once we have decided how many experimental conditions we
are going to include, we must decide how to assign each subject to
a particular condition. This decision is critically important; it is the
key to conducting sound research and being able to draw firm conclusions. It is the method of subject assignment that enables a researcher to eliminate many factors that would otherwise threaten the
internal validity of the results.

Random Assignment

In assigning subjects to experimental conditions we must follow a
procedure that ensures that each subject has an equal probability of
being in any of the conditions. Researchers call this procedure *randomization* or **random assignment of subjects to conditions.** (We
will shorten random assignment of subjects to conditions and simply
talk about **random assignment.**) Random assignment removes, from
both the experimenter and the subject, control over the condition to
which the subject is assigned. Manipulation of the independent variables and random assignment of subjects to different treatment conditions are the defining characteristics of experiments. We should
note here that although these aspects of experimentation are easier
in a laboratory, they are not restricted to laboratories.

As we noted, random assignment enables a researcher to
eliminate many factors that would otherwise threaten the internal
validity of the results. One of the ways it accomplishes this is by
controlling for subject variables. That is, it decreases the likelihood
that observed differences between subjects in the different conditions are due to preexisting differences between them.

When there are only two conditions in the experiment, random
assignment can be accomplished by a simple coin toss. When there
are more than two conditions, a table of random numbers or random
permutations can be used. These can be found in a text or they can
be generated by a computer.

One should be careful not to compromise random assignment,
even though an experimental procedure may take longer or be more
cumbersome than a control procedure. For example, an experimental

condition may require the presence of a confederate. When time is short or when the confederate is ill, the researcher may be tempted to test subjects in the control condition. The researcher should resist this temptation. Whenever true random assignment is compromised, there is the possibility of systematic bias.

An especially serious kind of bias can result when subjects assign themselves to particular experimental conditions. The pitfalls of asking subjects to choose which condition they prefer are so obvious that no experimenter would do it. However, the mortality factor, considered earlier, may create a subtle form of self-selection. Suppose that in Schachter's experiment subjects who were especially afraid of shocks refused to continue if they were assigned to the high anxiety condition. In this case, the only subjects left would be those for whom the threat of shocks had little impact.

Most experimenters are aware of the problems of different refusal rates in different experimental conditions. If, however, the refusal rate is the same in all conditions, some experimenters might be willing to assume that mortality is not a threat. This assumption is unsafe because there may be different reasons for refusal in the different conditions. Subjects in the severe shock condition of Schachter's experiment might refuse to go on because they were afraid. Subjects in the mild shock condition might refuse to go on because they were bored. A researcher should redesign an experiment if too many subjects refuse to complete it.

Single-Factor Designs

There are two basic types of experimental designs, **single-factor,** and **multi-factor** or factorial designs. Single-factor and multi-factor refer to the number of independent variables the experimenter manipulates. We will first describe two examples of single-factor designs, the *posttest-only control group* design and the *pretest–posttest control group* design. We will then describe one example of a multi-factor design, the *Solomon four-group* design. As we describe the designs we will consider threats to their internal and external validity.

Posttest-Only Control Group Design

In this design (see table 2.1) the researcher randomly assigns the subjects to the experimental and control groups. The researcher exposes subjects in the experimental condition to a treatment and then measures the dependent variable.

TABLE 2.1 Posttest-Only Control Group Design

	Manipulation	Posttest
Experimental	X	O
Control		O

Suppose an experimenter wanted to look at the television–aggression relationship using this design. A child who came to her laboratory would be randomly assigned to watch either a violent (experimental) or nonviolent (control) television program. To analyze the results the researcher would compare the posttest behavior of children in the experimental group and the control group.

Let us look at this design in more detail and see how it deals with threats to internal validity. Suppose that one day, there was a thunderstorm and the electricity flickered on and off. This might cause interruptions in the program and frustrate the children. Since the children are randomly assigned to the conditions as they come in, some of the rainy day children should be in the experimental group and some in the control group. If extraneous events like this occur, they should influence subjects in both conditions equally. Of course, if the experimenter had run the experimental condition on one day and the control condition on another day, history—in the form of the power interruptions—could have created a threat.

The problem of maturation has also been addressed by including the control condition. In devising an appropriate control condition, the experimenter had several alternatives. For instance, she could have allowed children in the control condition to continue playing with the toys or she could have asked them to do some unrelated task. Had the control children played with the toys they would have been able to move about freely while the experimental children sat still, watching television. This difference might have resulted in internal or maturational differences between the children. By having the children watch a nonviolent cartoon the experimenter kept the two conditions as similar as possible and minimized the threat of maturation.

Testing is not a threat. The researcher observed both groups for the same length of time and under the same conditions. Instrumentation is not a threat either because she randomly assigned the children to the conditions. Any changes in her ability to detect aggressive behavior would have affected observations in both conditions. If she had run all the children in the experimental condition first, instrumentation could have been a threat.

Sometimes a subject drops out of a study. As we said earlier, this is called mortality. A subject may leave for reasons that have nothing to do with the study; he might get sick or, in a long term study he might move. A subject may also leave for reasons related to the study (e.g., a boring control condition). Mortality for nonexperimental reasons should be taken care of by random assignment to conditions. For instance, we should not find that children are more likely to get sick in the experimental condition. However, mortality for experimental reasons could be a problem. If the nonviolent program were boring, the children might stop paying attention to it.

A design with no pretests makes some people uncomfortable when they first read about it. They ask, "What if differences existed between the groups before the experiment?" The answer is that selectivity should not be a problem if random assignment is properly done. To some extent, the statistical analysis of the results will indicate the likelihood that the difference is due to preexisting differences between the subjects. Suppose a statistical comparison between two conditions indicated a difference significant at the .05 level. This could be interpreted to mean that if people are randomly assigned properly and if there really is no treatment effect, then a difference at least this large would be expected five times out of a hundred.

Pretest–Posttest Control Group Design

In this design (see table 2.2) the researcher measures the dependent variable twice for both the experimental and control groups. During the period between the two measures the researcher exposes subjects in the experimental condition to some treatment.

Suppose an experimenter wanted to look at the television–aggression relationship using this design. She would observe the children. Then they would watch a violent (experimental) or nonviolent (control) television program. Finally, she would observe the children a second time. To analyze the results the researcher would compare the pretest and posttest behavior in both the experimental group and the control group.

Another version of the pretest–posttest design involves two (or more) experimental groups. Instead of (or in addition to) comparing the experimental and control groups, the researcher compares groups that have been exposed to different experimental treatments.

TABLE 2.2 Pretest–Posttest Control Group Design

	Pretest	Manipulation	Posttest
Experimental	O	X	O
Control	O		O

As with the posttest-only design, this design minimizes history, maturation, testing, instrumentation, and mortality for nonexperimental reasons. Random assignment eliminates the threat of selectivity. Even so, with this design the experimenter can examine the pretest scores to see if subjects in the two conditions differed in aggressive behavior before they watched the television cartoon. If random assignment was successful, there should be no differences.

The pretest–posttest control group design has both advantages and disadvantages. The main advantage of this design is its sensitivity to small changes brought about by the independent variable. Naturally, there are always differences among subjects before they appear for an experiment. Some of the children in our hypothetical study of television violence would be more aggressive than others. By obtaining information about such individual differences and incorporating it in the analysis of the results, we can obtain a more precise estimate of the effect of the independent variable.

The main advantage of this design is also its main disadvantage. There may be an interaction between testing and the intervention. The pretest, which provides information about individual differences, may also heighten subjects' awareness that they are being studied. This may lead them to pay more attention to their own behavior or convey to them the researcher's expectation that their behavior will change from the first test to the second. If this is the case, then the external validity of the experiment may be compromised. The effect of the independent variable may be limited to situations where subjects have been sensitized by the administration of a pretest.

One way to minimize the threat to external validity posed by a pretest is to allow sufficient time to elapse between the pretest and the manipulation of the independent variable. However, this solution may not be satisfactory. For instance, in an attitude change study the pretest might start people thinking about issues they had not thought about before. If enough time intervenes between the pretest and the experimental manipulation, the person may start noticing, for the first time, newspaper and magazine articles on the topic. This, of course, should apply equally to experimental and control subjects. However, if we want to generalize the results to a population that has not experienced the pretest, this design is unsatisfactory.

Comparing the Two Designs

Both the posttest-only control group design and the pretest–posttest control group design are the best designs available for single-factor experiments. The pretest is the only difference between the two. A pretest has certain advantages. First, we can check to ensure that randomization was effective. Second, if we look at changes in scores from pre- to posttest we are able to detect smaller effects of our manipulation. Incidentally, it is only when we include a pretest that we can properly talk about "changes."

On the other hand, when designing experiments we should not become sidetracked from the original purpose of the research. Usually, we are interested in the effect of the independent variable, not with the effect of the pretest. One way to avoid the problems created by using a pretest is to use the posttest-only control group design.

Should a pretest be included? The answer to this question will usually depend on the nature of the independent variable. However, there is no simple answer. Each researcher must decide for him or herself if the advantages of the pretest outweigh the disadvantages.

Multi-Factor Designs

In most research, the experimenter is interested in more than one independent variable. Higbee and Wells (1972) reviewed types of designs that appeared in psychology journals in 1969. They found that 9 percent of the studies used single-factor designs, 72 percent used multiple-factor designs, and 19 percent used designs of other kinds.

Multi-factor experiments provide information about the effects of each of the independent variables considered separately (**main effects**). In addition, they provide information about how the independent variables produce combined effects (**interaction effects**). Because of this, a single study with a multi-factor design has a major advantage over a sequence of simpler studies, each with a single-factor design.

Multi-factor designs are usually described in terms of the number of factors and levels of factors investigated. A 2×2 (described as a "two by two") design would have two factors with two levels each. A $2 \times 2 \times 2$ design would have three factors with two levels each. A 2×3 design has two factors, one with two levels and one with three.

Schwartz and Bless (1992) conducted a $2 \times 2 \times 2$ experiment. In Germany in 1990 there was a political scandal, referred to as the "Barschel Scandal." Schwartz and Bless were interested in whether this affected people's trust in politicians in general.

Half of their subjects, students at the University of Mannheim, Germany, were asked to recall the names of the three people involved in the scandal and then to rate the trustworthiness of these three politicians (specific) and politicians in general (general). The other half of the subjects were also asked to rate the two sets of politicians but without first being asked for the names of those involved in the scandal. Schwartz and Bless also manipulated the order of the ratings. Half of the subjects in each group did the specific ratings of trustworthiness first and then the general ones. The other half of the subjects did the general ratings first and then the specific ratings. The variables in the $2 \times 2 \times 2$ design are: (1) names asked or not, (2) order of rating, and (3) type of rating (specific or general). The last two factors were repeated measures on the same subjects.

When Schwartz and Bless looked at the ratings of trustworthiness, they found an interaction between whether the subjects were asked the names and whether the ratings were of the specific politicians or politicians in general. These ratings can be seen in figure 2.1. When subjects were not asked to name the politicians involved in the scandal there was little difference in the general and specific ratings. On the other hand, when they were asked for the names first, they rated the specific politicians as less trustworthy and politicians in general as more trustworthy.

The Solomon Four-Group Design

One multi-factor design is known as the Solomon four-group design (see table 2.3). This is simply a combination of the two single-factor designs that we considered earlier. In this design, two groups are given the experimental treatment and two are not. One of the two groups in each category is given a pretest. As with all of the other experimental designs we have described, the Solomon design depends on random assignment of subjects to conditions.

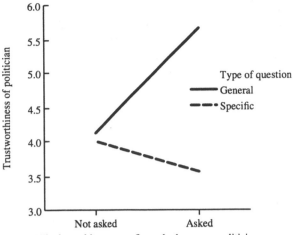

Whether subjects were first asked to name politicians
in scandal before rating trustworthiness.

FIGURE 2.1
Ratings of politicians derived from a multi-factor (2 × 2 × 2)
experimental design.

Copyright © 1992 Sage Publications. Based on Schwartz, N., &
Bless, H. (1992). Reprinted with permission of Sage Publications, Inc.

TABLE 2.3 Solomon Four-Group Design

	Pretest	Manipulation	Posttest
Group 1	X	X	X
Group 2	X		X
Group 3		X	X
Group 4			X

When the Solomon design is conceptualized as in table 2.4 the
two factors can be seen more clearly. The presence or absence of a
pretest is one factor and the presence or absence of an experimental
treatment is a second factor.

As you would expect, the Solomon design gathers all the information provided by the two simpler designs that it combines. To
determine whether taking a pretest has any effect on posttest scores,
we compare the posttest scores of people in groups 1 and 2 (row A)

TABLE 2.4 Solomon Four-Group Design as a 2 × 2 Multi-factor Experiment

		Treatment		
		Yes	No	
Pretest	Yes	1	2	A
	No	3	4	B
		C	D	

with those of people in groups 3 and 4 (row B). To determine if the experimental treatment has any effect on the posttest scores, we compare posttest scores of people in groups 1 and 3 (column C) with those of people in groups 2 and 4 (column D).

In addition to providing information about the main effects of pretest and treatment, the Solomon design tells us whether or not these two variables interact. This occurs if administering the pretest affects a subject's response to the experimental treatment.

To clarify the distinction between main effects and an interaction let us consider two possible outcomes when we use a Solomon design. To facilitate our discussion we will use as an example a study of safe sexual behavior in response to an educational campaign on the dangers of AIDS.

A researcher is interested in increasing high school students' knowledge of AIDS and changing their attitudes towards safe sex. However, she does not know what they already know nor what their attitudes are. She pretests the attitudes and knowledge of half of the students. Then she exposes half of these students and half of the students she did not pretest to an educational campaign. Finally, she measures all the students' attitudes toward and knowledge about AIDS. Let us consider two possible results: (1) two main effects—no interaction, and (2) two main effects and an interaction.

Two Main Effects—No Interaction
This outcome is shown in figure 2.2. On the posttest, subjects who received the pretest report safer sexual practices than do those who did not receive the pretest, regardless of whether or not they took part in the educational program. It is possible that the pretest started subjects thinking about the dangers of AIDS and that this alone was

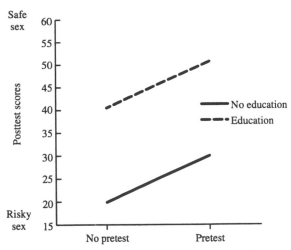

FIGURE 2.2
Two main effects but no interaction.

sufficient to cause a change in their behavior. The educational campaign has also had an effect regardless of whether or not the subjects took the pretest. Subjects who saw this campaign appear to have adopted safer sexual practices than have subjects who did not see the campaign.

In this experiment the effects of the pretest and the educational campaign are independent of each other. The campaign has exactly the same effect on people who were pretested as on people who were not pretested. In different language, the two independent variables add together to produce an effect but they do not interact with each other. You could say that their relationship is additive but not multiplicative.

Two Main Effects and an Interaction
This outcome is shown in figure 2.3. Overall, both the pretest and the educational campaign appear to have resulted in reports of safer sexual practices. When we examine the situation more closely, however, we can see that the effect of the campaign was greater among the pretested subjects than among those who were not pretested. In this case, the two independent variables interact with each other. They combine in a multiplicative fashion in influencing the dependent variable. When there is an interaction between two independent variables, we cannot specify the effect of either one without

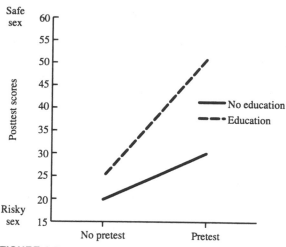

FIGURE 2.3
Two main effects and an interaction.

reference to the other. For example, if someone asked you about the effect of the educational campaign, you would have to answer, ''It depends on whether or not the people were pretested.''

The Solomon design eliminates virtually all of the threats to internal validity. It also is particularly useful for studying the effectiveness of various techniques for changing behavior. However, researchers do not use it often. There are several reasons for this. Most researchers do not think their pretest is likely to interact with their manipulation. If they do expect an interaction, they use a posttest–control group design. This is because they are interested in the impact of the manipulation, not the interaction with the pretest. The Solomon design requires twice as many subjects (and may take twice as long) as a posttest-only control group design. Finally, a researcher interested in two variables, *a* and *b,* may complicate the results drastically by using a Solomon design. In this case, a 2×2 design becomes a $2 \times 2 \times 2$ design. For a more advanced discussion of this design from a statistical perspective, see Braver and Braver (1988).

Threats to External Validity in Single- and Multi-Factor Designs

So far we have devoted most of our attention to threats to internal validity. We have seen how random assignment of subjects to treatment conditions—the mark of a true experimental design—helps to eliminate these threats. Random assignment, however, is little help in dealing with threats to the external validity or generalizability of an experiment. Indeed, as we will see later, in some cases it may reduce our ability to generalize the results of an experiment.

In the next section we will discuss three variables that threaten the external validity in social psychological studies: *artificiality, restricted subject populations,* and *subjects' knowledge that they are in an experiment.*

Artificiality

Nonpsychologists sometimes ask, "How can you generalize from the laboratory to 'real life'?" They are referring to the apparently artificial nature of much social psychological research.

As we have said before, one of the goals of an experimental design is to eliminate alternative explanations for the results. To accomplish this we try to isolate and manipulate only the variable in which we are interested. To isolate a variable, psychologists, like most other scientists, have found that at some stage in the investigation the variable must be studied in the laboratory.

Most variables we study occur in the real world in conjunction with other variables. Almost by definition, trying to isolate them— either in or outside of the laboratory—creates an artificial situation. This artificiality is a necessary part of the experimental process. Does this artificiality limit our ability to generalize to situations where the variables are not isolated? Does artificiality limit external validity?

In responding to the artificiality criticism of social psychology experiments Aronson and colleagues (1990) distinguished between **mundane realism** and **experimental realism.** Mundane realism refers to the extent to which an experimental situation resembles the world outside the laboratory. The greater the resemblance between an experimental situation and one which could exist outside the laboratory, the greater its mundane realism. An experiment in which a confederate, posing as a subject, asks a real subject for a date possesses a great deal of mundane reality—asking a person for a date is common behavior outside the laboratory.

Experimental realism exists when the subject believes that what is happening in the experiment is real and that his actions are influencing what is occurring. In general, as mundane realism increases, experimental realism increases. However, many experiments which lack mundane realism possess experimental realism.

Milgram (1963) performed an experiment in which the subject believed himself to be delivering shocks to another person. This experiment had little mundane reality—intentionally shocking a person is uncommon behavior outside the laboratory. Observers have noted, however, that Milgram's subjects were very caught up in what they were doing. They believed that they were really shocking and hurting another person and they often experienced great stress. These experiments had great experimental realism. To the extent that subjects are caught up in an experiment and believe what is happening, their responses are less likely to reflect simply an "artificial experimental situation."

Carlsmith, Ellsworth, and Aronson (1976) felt that when people criticize the artificiality of a laboratory experiment they are confusing mundane and experimental realism. They are judging experiments to be lacking mundane realism when it is experimental realism which determines our ability to generalize to the world outside of the laboratory.

Subject Population

Concern about the external validity of social psychological research often focuses on the restricted population from which research subjects are drawn. The subjects in most social psychological experiments are college students. From 1952 to 1972, the percent of studies using college students increased from 20 percent to 76 percent (Oakes, 1972). Can we generalize from this select portion of the population to the rest of the population?

The answer to this question depends on whether we want to make an **absolute** or a **relative generalization.** An example of an absolute generalization would be the statement, "Twenty-five percent of the population of North America believes in ghosts." We are saying exactly how many people in a population possess a particular characteristic, hold a certain belief, etc. As you will see when we discuss surveys, if we want to make an absolute generalization we would be making a mistake to survey simply one segment of the population be it college students, blacks, women, etc.

An example of a relative generalization would be the statement, "On average, children are more likely to believe in ghosts than are adults." We are not saying exactly how many children or adults believe in ghosts. We are saying that no matter where you go in North America (let's keep it local for now), if you talk to a child and you talk to an adult, the child is more likely to believe in ghosts than is the adult.

Most social psychological research leads to relative conclusions. Aronson and Mills (1959) had subjects undergo initiations of differing severity. Some had a severe initiation, some had a mild initiation, and some had no initiation. All of the subjects then listened to a group engaging in a dull, boring conversation. The subjects rated how interesting the conversation was and how much they would like to join the group. Subjects who underwent the severe initiation rated the conversation as more interesting than did subjects in the other two conditions. They were also more likely to want to join the group. Based on this study we can say that severe initiations result in greater attraction to a group than do less severe initiations.

In generalizing from the Aronson and Mills (1959) research to the world outside the laboratory, we can say that if two groups differ only in the severity of their initiation procedures, then the members of the group with the more severe initiation will probably be more attracted to their group. We may also be able to say, again all things being equal, that if a group increases the severity of its initiation, its members will be more strongly attracted to it.

There may, however, be occasions when we cannot make even relative generalizations. This occurs when the variables we are manipulating have different effects on different populations. When we discussed multi-factor experiments we introduced the concept of interactions. Two independent variables interact if we cannot predict the impact of one without knowing the level of the other. If two variables do not interact, we say they are independent. That is, we can predict the impact of one without knowing the level of the other. If our experimental variables are independent of population characteristics, our previous argument about relative generalizations holds. On the other hand, if the variables interact with population characteristics—that is, if they have different effects on different populations—we cannot make even relative generalizations.

Gergen (1973) has gone further to say that we may not even be able to make relative generalizations across time. That is, in thirty years it may be impossible to replicate the research results that we are obtaining today.

When the experimental variables and population characteristics are independent, the relative impact of different levels of the independent variable on the dependent variable will remain the same no matter what the population. If the impact of severity of initiation is independent of population, more severe initiations

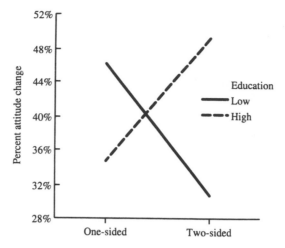

FIGURE 2.4
Attitude change as a function of type of argument
presentation and level of audience education.
From Hovland, Lumsdaine, and Sheffield (1949) with
permission of Princeton University Press.

should result in greater group attraction no matter what the population. It should be true for factory workers, office workers, college
students, or even college professors.

If on the other hand, population characteristics interact with
the independent variable then we may not be able to generalize to
different populations. In a classic experiment Hovland, Lumsdaine,
and Sheffield (1949) investigated the effect of one-sided versus two-
sided argument presentations on attitude change. Their subjects
were army soldiers. They found that the two-sided presentation was
more effective with better educated persons while the one-sided presentation was more effective with less educated ones. The results
might be diagrammed as in figure 2.4.[1]

The results of Hovland, Lumsdaine, and Sheffield's research
indicated that the argument variable (one-sided versus two-sided
presentation) interacts with education level. Had the study been
based only on college students, the researchers would probably have

---

1. Hovland, Lumsdaine, and Sheffield (1949) calculated the percent scores in the
following way:

| Percent who change | Percent who change | Net change in |
| in desired direction | − in opposite direction | − control condition |

drawn the conclusion that two-sided presentations were more effective at changing peoples' attitudes. Before we can make relative generalizations about the impact of one-sided versus two-sided presentations, we need to know the population to which we are generalizing.

So far, we have considered whether the results of research on college students can be generalized to noncollege students. Some people have gone further and questioned whether we can make a relative generalization to other college students. In many universities, students enrolled in introductory psychology courses are required to serve as subjects in a fixed number of experiments. Where this is not required, experimenters rely on volunteers solicited from courses onáthe campus or through newspaper advertisements. Do volunteers differ from the rest of the population in a manner which might interact with the experimental variable? Rosenthal and Rosnow (1969), after reviewing the literature, found that there were indeed personality differences between those who volunteered for experiments and those who did not. They concluded that we should not rely on volunteer subjects. However, their analysis of experiments in which both volunteer and nonvolunteer subjects were used failed to find any strong interactions or main effects related to volunteering.

Kruglanski (1973) argued that whether subjects are volunteers or nonvolunteers should not be of great concern to social psychologists. He first points out that people volunteer to participate in an experiment for a wide variety of reasons. There is no evidence to show that these reasons would systematically bias the subjects' responses. Kruglanski's second point is the one we made earlier. He, too, feels that Rosenthal and Rosnow failed to demonstrate that volunteers respond differently from nonvolunteers in experimental situations.

Hovland (1959) raised a related question—can we generalize from studies that use nonvolunteer subjects when, in real life, most people usually choose to be in or to avoid a situation. Hovland reviewed the results of laboratory and field research on attitude change. He pointed out that while laboratory studies have fairly consistently found attitude change following a communication, field surveys have usually not. Hovland attributed this difference to what he called the **captive audience** with which psychologists in the laboratory often deal. When a psychologist conducts an experiment on attitude change, or anything else, subjects are contacted and asked to participate in an experiment. They are given little or no information about the experiment itself. When they appear, they are exposed to the independent variable. In an attitude change experiment this might be a communication expounding a particular viewpoint. The subjects are a captive audience in the sense that they did not choose to hear the communication nor are they free to leave.

Contrast this with the population at large when a viewpoint is being expounded in print or on television. People choose whether to read or not to read, to listen or not to listen, to the communication. Hovland suggested that outside the laboratory people tend to expose themselves to communications with which they already agree and, therefore, attitude change is unlikely. On the other hand, the captive audience will probably include people who do not agree with the communication and some of these people may change their minds. Thus, in field research, experimenters usually deal with a voluntary subject population but in laboratory research, they do not.

We have discussed these issues at some length to show how complicated the question of external validity can be. Before we can say if a study has external validity we have to know the population to which we want to generalize and whether or not the independent variable interacts with population characteristics.

The Effects of Being Observed

Most people are careful to behave in a socially proper fashion when they think they are being observed. This is likely to be especially true if the setting is a social psychology experiment and the observers are researchers. People's behavior in this setting may be atypical. Individuals may try to help the experimenter by doing what they think he expects of them. They may try to act in a socially acceptable manner. If this is the case, then the results of the study may lack external validity. The threat to external validity caused by subjects' awareness that they are being studied is known as **reactivity.**

One obvious solution to the problem of reactivity is to study people's behavior without their being aware of it. Sometimes it will be necessary to deceive subjects to do this. Consider the following example.

Suppose a friend asks to borrow your new car while his is being repaired. Since he is a friend you are willing to lend him your car but you want to know how carefully he drives. One way to find out is to ask him to show you how he drives. Obviously, no matter how he normally drives, he will drive carefully because he wants to borrow your car. He will show you the socially acceptable way of driving. After driving with him you will still have little idea how he drives when you are not observing him.

If you wish to get a more accurate assessment of how your friend normally drives, you might ask him for a ride to the store while he still has his own car. Since he is "giving you a lift," your friend would be less likely to suspect that you are observing his driving behavior. You might then get a more accurate indication of his skills and degree of caution. Using a ruse to divert a person's attention from the behavior one is observing is a strategy that social psychologists frequently use in their experiments.

As noted in the discussion of ethical safeguards (chapter 1), several psychologists (e.g., Baumrind, 1985; Kelman, 1967) are concerned about use of deception in research designs. Deception can dehumanize subjects and may damage the self-concept of both subject and researcher. Both subject and researcher may also emerge with unfavorable views of psychology as a profession. To guard against this, the American Psychological Association (APA) and the Canadian Psychological Association (CPA) have strict ethical guidelines governing the use of deception in research. (The relevant guidelines are reproduced in appendix A.) In addition, virtually all colleges and universities in North America have ethical review committees with mandates to examine the ethics of any research with humans. This review is a required procedure before an experiment may begin. Despite precautions, there is some question about whether the impact of some kinds of deceptions can be fully eliminated afterwards.

Although social psychologists continue to use deception in their research (Christensen, 1988), most researchers try to minimize its use. Many are uncomfortable with the procedure but there does not yet appear to be a better alternative for avoiding reactivity. Today more social psychologists are exploring alternative procedures, some of which will be examined when we consider nonexperimental alternatives in chapter 5.

Summary

In an experiment the independent variable is manipulated and the dependent variable is measured. For us, the characteristics that define an experiment are the manipulation of the independent variable and the random assignment of subjects to the different treatment conditions. By randomly assigning subjects, researchers insure that on the average, differences between the groups—other than those caused by the independent variable—are minimized. Random assignment helps to minimize alternative explanations for the results and reduces threats to the internal validity of the design.

Threats to the internal validity of a research design include:

History—What appears to be the effect of an independent variable is really the effect of extraneous events or simply the passage of time.

Maturation—What appears to be the effect of an independent variable is really the effect of changes within the people being studied.

Mortality—What appears to be the effect of an independent variable is really the effect of people dropping out of the experiment before it is finished.

Selectivity—What appears to be the effect of an independent variable is really the effect of subjects being assigned to the experimental conditions in some biased fashion.

Testing—What appears to be the effect of an independent variable is the effect of the measurement and testing process itself.

Threats to the external validity of social psychological experiments include the artificiality of the testing situation. In addition, the restricted and homogeneous subject population (usually college students) used in social psychological experiments may also pose a threat to external validity.

Another threat to external validity is reactivity. Whether inside or outside the laboratory, people may respond differently if they know they are being observed. Social psychologists have resorted to deception to avoid the threat of reactivity. The use of deception raises serious ethical concerns for many social psychologists and is strictly governed by the ethical guidelines of both the American and Canadian Psychological Associations.

Experimental designs can be divided into single-factor and multi-factor designs. In single-factor designs, one independent variable is manipulated. The two single-factor designs—posttest-only and pretest–posttest—control for most of the threats to internal validity. The pretest–posttest design is more sensitive to small changes but has less external validity than does the posttest-only design.

In multi-factor designs two or more independent variables are manipulated. Multi-factor designs allow researchers to examine the separate effects of variables as well as the effects of interactions among them.

In this chapter we discussed general issues about the independent and dependent variables. In the next chapter we will discuss independent variables in more detail.

Manipulating the Independent Variable

Social psychologists often frame hypotheses using variables such as anxiety, schemas, arousal, cognitive consistency, aggression, conformity, cooperation, stereotypes, prosocial behavior, deindividuation, crowding, conflict, social pressure, and so on. For example, conformity will increase as social pressure increases; aggression will be more common under crowded conditions; deindividuated individuals will be less likely to engage in prosocial behavior. We call these variables **conceptual variables.** A researcher cannot directly test hypothetical relationships among conceptual variables. We need to specify how we will manipulate the independent variables and how we will measure the dependent variables. When we have set out these specifications, we say we have *operationally defined* the variables (**operational variables**). Both psychologists and philosophers of science have addressed the question of what constitutes an operational definition. When we use this term, we mean a statement or set of statements describing the procedures used to manipulate and/or measure the variable in question.

A researcher can operationalize conceptual variables in many different ways. Decisions on this matter are among the most critical that the researcher has to make. In this chapter and the next we will examine how researchers make these decisions. We will also examine how these decisions can affect the internal and the external validity of the experiment. The present chapter will deal with manipulations of independent variables. The next chapter will focus on problems related to the measurement of dependent variables.

We know that the independent variable is the hypothesized causal variable—the one the experimenter manipulates or varies. In deciding how to manipulate the independent variable, researchers typically have two goals in mind. The first is to achieve as close a match as possible between the conceptual variable and the operational variable. The second goal, closely related to the first, is to maximize the precision with which the manipulation can be carried out. We will consider each of these goals in turn as well as some of the obstacles that can make them difficult to realize.

Achieving a Close Match to the Conceptual Variable

Researchers often disagree about what constitutes the most appropriate operational definition of a conceptual variable. Consider, for example, Schachter's (1959) classic experiment on anxiety and affiliation described in chapter 2. To operationalize the conceptual variable of anxiety he manipulated subjects' expectations about the severity of electric shocks they were going to receive. Schachter told half of the subjects that the shocks would produce a mild tickling sensation. He told other subjects that the shocks would be severe but they would not cause any "permanent damage." He then asked subjects whether they wanted to wait alone or with other subjects while the experimenter set up the shock apparatus.

Schachter wanted to find out if anxiety about the shocks would make subjects want to affiliate with the other subjects. The results of his experiment revealed that people who anticipated severe shocks indicated a greater preference for waiting with others than did those who anticipated mild shocks.

Schachter thought the conceptual variable he had operationalized was *anxiety* but Sarnoff and Zimbardo (1961) thought that it was *fear*. Although people sometimes use the terms "fear" and "anxiety" interchangeably, Sarnoff and Zimbardo thought the terms should be distinguished. We usually define anxiety as a response to

TABLE 3.1 Mean Affiliation Scores: High Scores Indicate a Stronger Desire to Wait with Others

	High	Low
Fear	51	34
Anxiety	8	24

Based on Sarnoff, I. & Zimbardo, P. (1961) Anxiety, fear and social affiliation, in *Journal of Abnormal and Social Psychology, 62* (pp. 356–363).

a stimulus that poses no direct physical threat to the person. Fear, on the other hand, is a response to an identifiable, physical danger. Sarnoff and Zimbardo operationalized anxiety by asking subjects to put objects in their mouths. In the high anxiety condition they had to spend two minutes sucking on objects associated with infant oral behavior, for instance, baby pacifiers, baby bottles, and breast shields. Subjects in the low anxiety condition merely had to put objects such as whistles, kazoos, and balloons in their mouths for ten seconds. Sarnoff and Zimbardo operationalized fear by threatening other subjects with shocks.

The results of the Sarnoff and Zimbardo study are shown in table 3.1. The results of the fear condition replicate those of Schachter. People who were highly fearful wanted to affiliate or wait with others more than did people who were less fearful. However, when we look at Sarnoff and Zimbardo's operationalization of anxiety, we see that the results point in the opposite direction. People who were highly anxious preferred to wait alone rather than with others. The difference between Sarnoff and Zimbardo's results and those of Schachter can be attributed to the different definitions used. Together these two studies show how important it is to have a clear definition of the conceptual variable before trying to operationalize and manipulate it.

Maximizing the Precision of the Experimental Manipulation

Ideally, the independent variable is the only variable that varies systematically from one experimental condition to another. In practice, however, an experimental manipulation almost always includes variables besides those the researcher intended. Two additional variables, experimenter bias and demand characteristics, can seriously undermine the researcher's ability to draw appropriate conclusions from the results. **Experimenter bias** refers to the unintentional ways (as opposed to cheating, etc.) in which an experimenter, as part of the experimental environment, can influence the outcome of an experiment. **Demand characteristics** refer to cues (other than those conveyed by the experimenter) that let subjects know what behaviors are expected of them.

Experimenter Bias

Rosenthal (1963) was the first social psychologist to study experimenter bias. He and his colleagues demonstrated the effects of experimenter bias on such diverse subject populations as worms in a runway, rats in a maze, humans in a laboratory, and teachers in classrooms.

To demonstrate how experimenter bias could affect a rat's behavior, Rosenthal and Fode (1963a) asked students in a psychology laboratory course to train rats in a maze, each experimenter training one rat. Half of the rats to be trained had their cages marked to indicate that they were "maze bright" and half had cages indicating they were "maze dull." The signs were placed randomly on the cages. When the results were tabulated it appeared that the rats that had "bright" signs learned faster than those that had "dull" signs. Further analysis showed that the difference could not be attributed to dishonesty or errors in scorekeeping on the part of the experimenters.

In another study Rosenthal and Fode (1963b) gave different experimenters different expectations about the characteristics that their (human) subjects would attribute to a man whose photograph they viewed. Rosenthal told half the experimenters that subjects would think the person in the photograph was successful. He told other experimenters that subjects would think the person was unsuccessful. Rosenthal found that experimenters tended to obtain results that were consistent with their experimentally-induced expectations.

In most situations it is not clear, even to the experimenters, how they are conveying the bias to the subjects. Thus, experimenter bias is difficult to prevent. One way of minimizing the bias is to keep the experimenters unaware of the hypothesis being tested. There are two reasons this procedure may not be entirely satisfactory. First, people conducting experiments are usually student researchers. It is unfair to deprive them of part of their learning experience. Second, if we do not tell experimenters the hypothesis, they may formulate their own hypotheses about the purpose of the experiment and bias the results in that way.

Another way to minimize experimenter bias is to standardize all aspects of the interaction between the experimenter and the subject. For example, the researcher can present instructions as well as experimental manipulations in written form, or on audio- or video-tape. Alternatively, most of the experiment can be conducted by a computer. The computer can randomly assign the subject to an experimental condition, present the instructions and experimental manipulations on the screen, record the subject's responses, and conclude by thanking the subject warmly for participating.

Where we cannot standardize all aspects of the experimenter-subject interaction, the **double-blind procedure** provides the best protection against experimenter bias. When this procedure is followed, neither the subject nor the experimenter is aware of the experimental condition to which the subject has been assigned.

Imagine an experiment in which a researcher wants to study the effect of different kinds of problems on group problem solving. The independent variable is a type of problem—logical, mathematical, or spatial. The dependent variable is how the group goes about solving the problem. Particularly, do they work as a group or does each member of the group work individually at the problem? Each group gets one problem to solve.

Before the experiment starts, the researcher randomizes the order of the three kinds of problems and puts each one into an unmarked envelope. Before the subjects appear for the experiment he places one of the envelopes on the table around which the subjects will be seated. He does not know what type of problem is in the envelope. After the subjects are seated he explains that their task is to solve the problem in the envelope.

Since the dependent measure is whether people work alone or together, the researcher does not have to listen to their conversation (perhaps it would be recorded for later analysis). He would leave the room and go to an observation room before the group starts its task. To record the dependent measure he would observe the group and rate whether the members are working alone or together.

The subjects are blind to experimental condition. They do not know what the different conditions are nor to which one they have been assigned. The researcher is also blind to condition. He does not know, at any stage, under which condition the subjects are operating. Thus, his expectations cannot influence the results. This is a double-blind design.

When it is not possible to keep the experimenter blind for the entire experiment, it is best to keep him or her blind as long as possible. In the example of the pretest–posttest control group experimental design that we considered earlier, the experimenter pretested the children before they were randomly assigned to conditions. Thus, when she first observed the children playing with the toys, she did not know whether the children would be seeing a violent or nonviolent cartoon. She could not treat the two groups differently.

Demand Characteristics

Orne (1962) was the first social psychologist to investigate demand characteristics. Orne suggested that most research subjects pay careful attention to cues in the research situation that signal the appropriate behavior. As a result, their behavior may be influenced not by the independent variable but by those cues that tell them how to look good or how to confirm the experimenter's hypothesis.

By manipulating environmental cues in the research situation, Orne demonstrated the strong influence that demand characteristics can have on experimental results. The early research on people's reactions to sensory deprivation provides an example. This research indicated that when subjects were placed in dark, sound-proof rooms for a few hours, they often reported hallucinations, and their behavior and thought processes deteriorated. Orne and Scheibe (1964) wondered if these subjects were reacting to sensory deprivation or to demand characteristics. To find out, they conducted a sensory deprivation study that was unlike most of the earlier ones.

In Orne and Scheibe's study, subjects waited in a well-lit "deprivation room" with two comfortable chairs, ice water, and a sandwich. The subjects could add columns of numbers if they felt like it. Although the subjects did not know the duration of the experiment, it was to last for only four hours.

For subjects in the experimental condition, the situation included a series of special release forms, a tray with drugs and instruments, and a red "panic" button to press if the "isolation" became too much. In the control condition, these cues were absent. Orne and Scheibe found that subjects in the experimental condition showed a decrement in motor performance and exhibited perceptual aberrations. This was the same behavior shown by subjects in normal sensory deprivation experiments. The subjects in the control condition, however, showed no ill effects from their experience. Orne and Scheibe concluded that the presence of the forms and the red button made subjects in the experimental condition think that in this situation it was appropriate to show an adverse reaction and they behaved accordingly. After the Orne and Scheibe study was published, research on sensory deprivation decreased markedly.

Of course, subjects will not always behave in strict accordance with demand characteristics. For example, if the demand characteristics make subjects think the researcher expects them to perform poorly, they may make a special effort to perform well (cf., Sigall, Aronson, & Van Hoose, 1970). From the experimenter's perspective, however, behavior in accordance with demand characteristics and behavior that is intentionally in the opposite direction are equally troublesome. In either case, the influence of the real independent variable is obscured.

Orne has suggested what he calls **quasi-control** groups as a way of determining, after the experiment, whether demand characteristics were operating. There are two quasi-control procedures. One involves explaining the procedure of the experiment to a new sample of subjects (quasi-control subjects), showing them the experimental material, and telling them what the real subjects had to do. The quasi-control subjects are asked why they think the experiment is being done. They are also asked what they think the experimenter's hypotheses are. If quasi-control subjects can figure out what the experimenter's hypotheses are, then it is likely that the real subjects might have as well. Thus, demand characteristics might account for the results. However, one can only suspect that this is so. The experimenter cannot make a determination with certainty.

The other quasi-control procedure involves including an experimental condition in which one group of subjects is exposed to the independent variable while another group of subjects is not. This group is instructed to act as if the experimenter exposed them to the independent variable. A second experimenter who is unaware of which subjects are "real" and which are simulating then assesses their behavior. If the behavior of the real and simulating subjects cannot be distinguished, then it is possible that demand characteristics are producing the results.

Orne and Evans (1965) used a simulation procedure to determine whether demand characteristics could account for the antisocial behavior of hypnotized subjects. Early researchers (Rowland, 1939, and Young, 1952) found that subjects who were hypnotized would perform antisocial acts that might harm themselves or others. Control subjects, who were not hypnotized, refused to perform these acts.

Rowland (1939) asked hypnotized subjects to pick up a large, active, rattlesnake. Three of the four subjects reached in for the snake. In response to the experimenter's request two other hypnotized subjects threw what they thought was sulfuric acid in an assistant's face. Young (1952) replicated Rowland's results. Seven out of eight hypnotized subjects carried out suggestions that they pick up a snake and throw nitric acid at an assistant. In both the Rowland and the Young studies, subjects who were not hypnotized refused to do either of the tasks.

Orne and Evans (1965) replicated these early experiments. The experimenter hypnotized some subjects and told others to act as if they had been hypnotized. A second experimenter did not know which subjects had been hypnotized and which were simulating hypnosis. He asked the subjects to engage in the antisocial behavior. Because he did not know who was hypnotized, he treated both groups of subjects alike. They were both exposed to the same demand characteristics. All of the hypnotized subjects tried to carry out all of the tasks they were asked to do. However, all six simulation subjects also tried to carry out the tasks the second experimenter asked them to do. Based on their behavior, they could not be distinguished from the hypnotized subjects.

Quasi-controls are time consuming and the results are often unclear. Even if we discover that demand characteristics could have been operating, it does not mean they were responsible for the results. As Orne and Evans (1965, p. 199) stated, "No conclusions can be drawn from the present investigation about the potential use of hypnosis to induce antisocial behavior." This is why many social psychologists ignore the problem of demand characteristics.

In the preceding sections we have tried to show some of the difficulties involved in operationalizing the independent variable. We first talked about achieving a close match between the conceptual and operational variable. We then discussed the effect experimenter bias and demand characteristics can have on the precision of the experimental manipulation. If experimenter bias or demand characteristics are operating, any changes in the dependent measure will be difficult to interpret.

We must keep in mind, however, that we are not interested in the operational variable, per se. It is the underlying conceptual variable that has theoretical importance. For example, if we tried to manipulate people's moods by showing them either a comic or tragic film, the particular films used would not be of much interest. In fact, if we could obtain the results with only two particular films, the results would have little importance.

The problem of generalizing from the operational to the conceptual variable is similar to the problem of external validity. However, rather than generalizing to other populations or other times, we want to generalize to other manipulations of the conceptual variable. We call the ability to generalize from the operation to the concept, **conceptual validity.**[1]

As with internal and external validity, there are several threats to the conceptual validity of an experiment. We have discussed some of these. If one does not achieve a close match to the conceptual variable, the results will lack conceptual validity. Both experimenter bias and demand characteristics can threaten the conceptual validity of the results.

One way to determine the conceptual validity of experimental results is to carry out what are called **conceptual replications.** By conceptual replications we mean experiments that investigate the same conceptual variable but operationalize this variable differently.

Conceptual Replications

Sometimes conceptual replications "work" in the sense that the new experiment with a different operationalization of the independent variable produces results that are similar to those of the original experiment. Other times, the attempt to replicate does not work. Both outcomes are informative but in different ways. Let us consider two examples.

Destructive Obedience: A Replication That Worked

In a well-known series of experiments Milgram (1964) put subjects in an unpleasant situation by instructing them to administer increasingly painful and even dangerous electric shocks to another subject. The experimenter told subjects that they were participating in a learning experiment. He told them that the shocks were necessary for the researchers to learn about the effects of punishment on learning. In fact the "victim" in this situation was a confederate of

---

1. Cook and Campbell (1979) call this *construct validity*. We will reserve this term for the dependent variable, as you will see in the next chapter.

Milgram's who received no shocks. Nevertheless, from the subject's point of view the situation was very realistic and apparently most subjects believed they were administering actual shocks.

To his surprise, Milgram discovered that most subjects continued to administer what they thought were painful shocks despite screams of pain from the other person. To Milgram, the results demonstrated how difficult it is for a person to disobey instructions that come from someone in a position of recognized authority. Note, however, that such a general conclusion carries with it the assumption that the experimenter-subject relationship in a psychology experiment is similar to other kinds of relationships between persons of different status and power. Would Milgram have obtained the same results if he had operationalized his variables in a different way? A field experiment conducted by some doctors and nurses in a hospital setting (Hofling et al., 1966) sheds some light on this question.

Hofling and colleagues arranged to have the nurse who was in charge of a hospital ward receive a phone call from a doctor. The doctor instructed her to administer some medication to a patient on the ward. Several things about this situation were amiss.

> (a) Although the doctor's name appeared on the list of doctors associated with the hospital, the doctor was not known personally to the nurse. That is, she did not recognize his voice.
> (b) The administration of medication to patients without written orders from a doctor was against hospital policy.
> (c) The amount of medication that the doctor was ordering was four times the usual dose and twice the maximum daily dose. This information about dosages was clearly marked on the bottle of medication.

The researcher described this scenario to off-duty nurses and student nurses. All but one said that if they were in that situation they would refuse to administer the medication. However, of the nurses actually faced with the situation, only one refused to comply with the doctor's instructions. An observer had to intercept the rest before they could inflict damage on the hapless patient.

The study by Hofling and colleagues (1966) can be considered a conceptual replication of the studies by Milgram.[2] Both research efforts explored the limits of destructive obedience. At the operational

---

2. Although the Hofling study appears to us to be a conceptual replication of Milgram's research, Hofling and colleagues were apparently unaware of Milgram's work when they carried out their study.

level, however, almost everything about the studies is different. Because of these operational differences, the similarity of the results in the two studies increases our confidence in their conceptual validity.

Selective Learning: Replications That Did Not Work

What conclusions can one draw when the results of a second study do not confirm those of an earlier one? This happened to researchers studying the relationship between attitudes and learning.

In an early study, Levine and Murphy (1943) examined subjects' memory rates for procommunist and anticommunist material. They discovered that people recalled more of the material that supported their own views than material that opposed their views. This phenomenon became known as "selective learning."

After the publication of Levine and Murphy's study, several researchers attempted to replicate their findings. Because the issue of communism was no longer topical, investigators chose such issues as racial integration (Brigham & Cook, 1969; Waly & Cook, 1966) and American involvement in Vietnam (Greenwald & Sakumura, 1967). Their efforts to replicate the selective learning effect were usually unsuccessful.

When researchers attempt to explain unsuccessful conceptual replications, they usually focus first on differences in the ways the conceptual variables were operationalized. In the case of the selective learning research, one difference was the attitudinal issues used. Levine and Murphy had demonstrated selective learning using the issue of communism. Later investigators who failed to replicate most often used the issue of racial integration. Levine and Murphy's subjects may have been more familiar with the issue of communism or may have felt more strongly about it than was the case for later subjects on the issue of racial integration. Perhaps familiarity and strong feelings are necessary conditions for the occurrence of selective learning.

There are many possible explanations for a failure to replicate and all of them need to be tested empirically before we can reach a final conclusion about the original findings. As failures to replicate accumulate, researchers will try to match more and more closely the conditions of the original study. Eventually, if the failures continue, research in the area will taper off and researchers will turn their attentions to more reliable phenomena. This appears to be what has happened to selective learning.

Few things generate as much research as does controversy. In science, few things are as controversial as a failure to replicate a published result. Sometimes the failure is clear-cut—the obtained result is directly counter to the published one. Other times, the result is ambiguous. The result takes the same direction as the earlier one, but does not reach statistical significance. When conflicting results accumulate in an area of the scientific literature, as they did with the selective learning phenomenon, there is a need for some method of weighing the individual bits of evidence and reaching a decision about the most reasonable conclusion.

In 1984 Rosenthal discussed a method called **meta-analysis** for comparing the results of several studies. Roberts (1985) used meta-analysis to look at thirty-eight studies of selective learning, including Levine and Murphy's original study (1943). He concluded that there is evidence for the selective learning/recall effect, but the effect was relatively small. We will consider meta-analytic methods in more detail in a later chapter.

Checking on the Manipulation

What happens when an experiment fails to produce a predicted result? The researcher may not be able to tell whether the theory that generated the prediction is incorrect or whether the manipulation of the independent variable was ineffective. To facilitate interpretation of results, many researchers incorporate measures into the experiments to assess the effectiveness of the manipulation of the independent variable. This is referred to as **check(ing) on the manipulation.**

Researchers may check the manipulation in a study run before the experiment, a **pilot study,** or they may check it during the experiment. For example, during Schachter's experiment on anxiety and affiliation, he asked subjects how they felt about being shocked. Schachter reported that subjects in his high-anxiety condition expressed much greater dislike about being shocked than subjects did in the low-anxiety condition. In addition, almost 19 percent of the subjects in the high-anxiety condition refused to continue but none of the subjects in the low-anxiety condition refused. Schachter cited both these findings as evidence for the effectiveness of his manipulation of anxiety.

Some researchers feel that the extra time and extra subjects make pilot studies uneconomical. They prefer to follow Schachter's example and check the manipulation during the actual experiment. One disadvantage to Schachter's procedure, however, is that the check on the manipulation may itself affect the dependent measure. For example, the check on the manipulation may draw subjects' attention to the manipulation. This may make their behavior more susceptible to demand characteristics.

One way to eliminate the influence of the check of the manipulation on the dependent measure is to check the manipulation at the end of the experiment, after obtaining all other measures. This is sometimes an attractive alternative but there are at least two problems with it. First, the procedure used to measure the dependent variables may affect the response on the manipulation check. Second, by the end of the experiment, the subject may not remember how he felt earlier when the experimental manipulation was introduced.

Another way to check the manipulation in an experiment is to include *check conditions* in the experimental design and to assign subjects randomly to these conditions during the experiment. The only difference between a pilot study and this check-condition procedure is that in the former case you assess the manipulation before the experiment and in the latter case you assess it during the experiment. The check-condition procedure has an advantage. Because the researcher randomly assigns subjects to the condition during the experiment, time of testing does not confound the results. The pilot study procedure has the advantage that the experimenter may discover problems with the manipulation early enough to rectify the situation.

Finally, in deciding how to operationalize the independent variable, the experimenter also must consider whether the manipulation used will facilitate the measurement of the dependent variable or whether it will make such measurements more difficult. In the next chapter we will consider the problems of measurement.

Summary

When a researcher plans an experiment, she wants to achieve a close match between the conceptual variable (e.g., anxiety) and the operational variable (e.g., telling people they will get shocked). She also wants to insure that the independent variable is the only variable that changes systematically from one experimental condition to another. Two variables that may be unintentionally varied are experimenter bias and demand characteristics. Experimenter bias refers to the ways in which an experimenter can unintentionally influence the outcome of an experiment. Demand characteristics refer to cues (other than those conveyed by the experimenter) that tell subjects what behaviors are expected of them.

Researchers are usually not interested in the operational variable, per se. It is the underlying conceptual variable that has theoretical importance. We have called the ability to generalize from the operation to the concept, "conceptual validity." One way to determine the conceptual validity of experimental results is to carry out conceptual replications. These are experiments that investigate the same conceptual variable but operationalize it differently.

If an experiment does not turn out the way the researcher expected, the hypothesis may be incorrect, or the manipulation of the independent variable may not have been effective. To distinguish between these two alternatives, researchers assess the effectiveness of the manipulation. They do this by checking on the manipulation during the course of the experiment.

In this chapter we discussed independent variables. In the next chapter we will discuss dependent variables.

4

The Dependent Variable

Types of Dependent Measures   **Measuring the Dependent Variable**
    Reliability
    Validity

Types of Dependent Measures

In general, dependent measures used to test the dependent variable can be divided into **obtrusive** and **unobtrusive** measures (Webb, Campbell, Schwartz, & Secrest, 1966). These are also referred to as **reactive** and **nonreactive** measures. When we ask people to respond in some way, to answer direct questions, or to make a choice from a set of alternatives we are using an obtrusive, reactive measure. People become aware that some aspect of their behavior is being studied and recorded. When we use unobtrusive measures people are not aware that they are being observed. The researcher does not approach people directly. Instead she observes their behavior and measures it from a distance.

Let us consider some of these ideas further with an example. Imagine that, as the director of a zoo, you want to find out how popular your different exhibits are. You decide to stop departing visitors and ask them to rank the exhibits according to how much they enjoyed them. When we use reactive measures like this, people may respond with "socially desirable" answers. These are responses that portray them personally in a positive light—that make them look good. As director of the zoo, you might well find that people report greatest enjoyment of the new exhibit with information about animals and the ecological dangers of rain-forest destruction.

Imagine now that you decide to measure the popularity of the different exhibits with a nonreactive, unobtrusive method. You ask the zoo custodians to make periodic counts of the number of people at each exhibit. When you tally the counts you find that the ecology-information exhibit attracted few visitors but large numbers watched the monkeys mating. Not surprisingly, no one mentioned this in the personal interviews.

When you use nonreactive, unobtrusive methods people are less likely to be aware that they are being studied and less likely to react to the measurement process itself. Nonreactive measures are less vulnerable to the systematic bias of social desirability that we discussed earlier.

On the other hand, nonreactive measures may involve costly, long-term observations. We also may have to demonstrate their connection to the underlying conceptual variable. This link may be less apparent than with reactive measures. In addition, nonreactive measures may be susceptible to other kinds of systematic biases. In our example, the monkey exhibit might be close to the food vendors or the public washrooms, and this factor might account for the many people it attracted.

When researchers consider using unobtrusive measures in an experiment they must also consider how they will manipulate the independent variable. If the manipulation is obtrusive it may prove difficult to have an unobtrusive measure of the dependent variable. Bochner (1971) used an unobtrusive measure of white Australians' attitudes toward aborigines. Racial attitudes are particularly susceptible to social desirability—people are rarely willing to admit to racial prejudice. To investigate subjects' attitudes, Bochner used a method he calls ''Street theater.'' At different times he had an aboriginal or a white girl walk a small dog through a park. The dependent variable was the number of times that members of the general public (all of whom were white) smiled, nodded at, or spoke to either girl during a specified period of time. Bochner classed these as ''encouragements.'' He found that the white girl received 50 encouragements while the aboriginal girl received only 18.

Our examples of unobtrusive measures have all involved watching people behave. Another type of unobtrusive measure comes from archival data. These are data about people collected by governments, businesses, etc. Examples of archival data would include things like court records of convictions, quantity of beer sold by stores, and titles of books stolen from the library. In chapter 5 we will present a study that used police records to see if publishing shoplifters' names reduced the number of people arrested for shoplifting.

There are ethical concerns about observing people's behavior when they are not aware that they are being observed. Do we invade people's privacy when we study them without their knowledge? To some extent the answer depends on who the people are and where and how we study them. For example, few people would argue that Bochner's study of people in a park was an invasion of privacy. But consider a different example. Many stores use closed-circuit television cameras and monitors to discourage shoplifting. Imagine that you were able to persuade the owner of such a store to let you review the videotapes at the end of each day in order to study how people behave in that kind of situation. Would you be invading those people's privacy?

Even when people in groups are aware they are being studied, the question of invasion of privacy sometimes arises when the results of the study are published. In most cases authors try to conceal or disguise the identities of the research participants, and this works fairly well for readers who were not closely connected with the research. But for the people involved in the research and the participants themselves, such disguises will not be effective.

Some of the members of the street gangs that Whyte (1943) studied apparently read *Street Corner Society* when it was published and not everyone was happy with the way they were portrayed. Although Whyte had changed the names, this didn't prevent the people from recognizing themselves and each other. Whyte returned to Cornerville after the book was published and talked to some of the members about their reactions. His account of this return visit became an appendix to later editions of his book.

Despite the susceptibility of questionnaires and interviews to the threat of reactivity, they are commonly used in experiments. There are several reasons for that popularity. Such measures are quick and easy to carry out. In addition, they usually have a certain **face validity.** That is, there appears to be a close match between the conceptual variable and the one we operationalize in the questions. What better way, for example, to find out how popular a zoo exhibit is than by asking visitors, "How much did you enjoy the exhibit on ———?" or "Which exhibit would you like to spend more time at if you return another day?" However, unobtrusive (nonreactive) measures provide an alternative that should be considered more often.

Measuring the Dependent Variable

As we saw in the last section, when investigators operationalize the independent variable, they strive to match the conceptual variable as closely as possible and to maximize the precision with which they can carry out the manipulation. In operationalizing the dependent variable, similar goals are important. However, precision of measurement rather than precision of manipulation takes precedence. Two important concepts to take into account in measurement are reliability and validity.

When we talk about the **reliability** of a measuring instrument (any measuring instrument) we are talking only about its repeatability, not its accuracy. A weight scale that consistently shows one person's weight as 300 kilograms and another person's weight as 400 kilograms, day after day, is a reliable weight scale. Whether or not the scale shows the correct weight is a different question, that of **validity.** Validity refers to the accuracy of a measure. A reliable instrument may or may not be valid but an unreliable instrument can clearly not be valid.

The process of measurement involves assigning a number or score to an object. The intent is to assign a score that reflects the true value of some characteristic that the object possesses. Unfortunately, the score a researcher obtains will often reflect systematic bias and random error. Consider the following equation.

Observed score = True score + Systematic bias + Random error

As this equation indicates, the score that results from the measurement process will, in general, be influenced by three different components.

Any variable that exerts a consistent influence on each score in a set contributes to what we call **systematic bias.** By consistent we mean it moves most people's score in the same direction. The amount of movement may vary from person to person, but the direction of movement is the same. Thus, the mean overall effect is not equal to zero. Systematic bias influences the validity of the measure. Experimenter bias and demand characteristics are examples of variables exerting a consistent bias.

Any variable that exerts an influence but in a direction that may vary from subject to subject, with time of day, etc. is called **random error.** Random errors vary in both size and direction but the mean overall effect is equal to zero. Random error influences the reliability of a score.

Let us consider a concrete example of how these influences might work. Suppose you want to measure the width of a doorway in your home. It is important that you get an accurate measure of the true width, so you ask twenty-five people to measure it too. You plan to average all of their scores.

You let each of the people use your old tape measure. However, without your knowledge, the first inch was cut off by your little brother. Further, the numbers on the tape measure are not easy to read, and the light in the doorway is not very good.

The missing inch on the tape measure will cause a systematic bias. It is systematic because everyone who uses the tape measure will arrive at a measure that is an inch longer than the true door width.

The poor light and the numbers that are hard to read will lead to random error. Some people may lean one way to see the numbers, others may lean the other way. Some may squint, others may not. Each of these methods of viewing will lead each of the people to see the numbers slightly differently. Some people may see the mark above the true measure, some may see the mark below the true measure. These errors, however, should average out to zero. That is, they should not exert a consistent directional influence on the estimates.

In the case of any single measurement, the influence of the true score, systematic bias, or random error can be zero. The relative contributions of the three components will determine both the reliability and the validity of the measurement.

Imagine a pie divided into three segments, one representing the influence of the true value, one representing systematic bias, and one representing random error. A scale is valid to the extent that a score reflects the true value (see figure 4.1). In some cases, however, the true value may contribute little or nothing. In such cases the measurement process will not be valid—it may reflect only systematic bias and/or random error (see figure 4.2).

When systematic bias or random error heavily influence the measurement score, it means that we are measuring something other than what we intended to measure. In social psychology there are several variables that can systematically bias our measurements. One such variable is social desirability. In responding to questionnaires or interview questions, people may give answers that they think will make them appear in a favorable light. What we may then be measuring is people's motivation to impress the person conducting the interview.

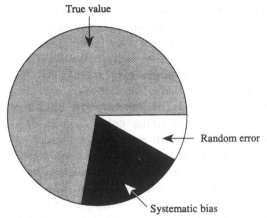

FIGURE 4.1
True value contributes heavily to score.

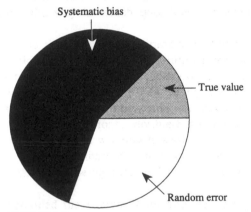

FIGURE 4.2
True value contributes little to score.

Reliability

The true value of a variable and the systematic biasing effects of other variables may remain constant. However, the influence of random error will vary from one measurement to the next. When the random error is negative, the score will underestimate the true value. When the random error is positive, the score will overestimate the true value. Random errors are assumed to be normally distributed around the zero point.

Of the three influences on measurement, the random error component is the only one that is assumed to vary. This fact makes it possible for us to estimate the error it contributes. We do this by examining the variability of the scores we obtain when we measure something on repeated occasions or in different ways. The more variable the scores, the more random error there must be in our method of measurement. The more random error there is, the less reliable the measure.

Because random error is normally distributed around the zero point, its *average* influence over many measurements will approach zero. Thus, it is always a good idea to measure a variable more than once and to average the scores we obtain. The average of several scores will usually be more reliable than any single score.

The advantage of repeated measurements is even greater when we use different methods of measurement. This is because different methods will, in general, be susceptible to different sources of systematic bias. It is likely that some of these sources of bias will be positive and others negative. Thus, the average of the scores obtained with different methods will be less biased than will any single score.

Let us return to our example of the zoo director. Remember that two measures were used, a reactive questionnaire and a nonreactive counting of people at the different exhibits. Remember too that the results of the two measures didn't agree. In response to the reactive question people said they were interested in the exhibit on damage to the rain-forest. However, it was the monkeys that drew the biggest crowds.

Which measure of popularity should the zoo director use? Before deciding, it would be a good idea to repeat both measurement methods several times on several days to see if the results are consistent. The degree of consistency in the results for each measure provides information about each measure's reliability. If only one of the two measures proves to be reliable, then the zoo director's choice is obvious.

If both measures are reliable, the director might then calculate the correlation between them. A significant positive correlation would indicate that one or more common factors influenced the two measurement methods. It could be that the same systematic biasing factor is influencing both methods. However, if the methods are sufficiently different, this is unlikely. It is more likely that the common factor is the true variable (exhibit popularity) that the director is trying to measure. In this case, both measures would have some validity and the best strategy would be to average the two measures to get a single score. We will discuss some methods for assessing validity later in this chapter.

Finally, if each of the two measurement methods is reliable but there is no significant correlation between them, the zoo director should probably look for a third measure of exhibit popularity and follow the sequence of steps that we have outlined. (Curiosity might lead the director to find out what the two measures were really measuring.)

We concluded earlier that we can enhance the reliability of measurement by measuring a variable several times in several different ways and averaging the results. In the next section we describe a few examples of the ways that social psychologists follow this procedure.

Inter-rater Reliability

When we use the **inter-rater reliability** method, two or more judges observe and rate the same behavior. The more consistent their ratings, the more confident the researchers can be that the ratings are reliable.

Let us say we suspect that lonely and nonlonely people act differently in social interactions. To test this possibility, we videotape many different people in a variety of social interactions. Then we ask two judges to indicate if they think the person was lonely or not. Before we can analyze the behavior in detail we must be sure that our judges agree on their ratings. (Remember that we are not yet concerned with whether the people actually are lonely—that is the question of validity.)

There are two ways to measure agreement between judges. We can look for how much absolute agreement there is between them or we can examine relative agreement by correlating their ratings. If the judges make the ratings on a nominal scale, we look for the amount of absolute agreement between them. If they make the ratings on an interval scale, we would normally use the correlation method. In this example, the judges were using a nominal scale (lonely versus not-lonely) so we assess their consistency by measuring the absolute agreement between them. Examining table 4.1 with this criterion in mind, we see that the judges agree on four (80 percent) of the five cases.

Suppose that we had asked the judges to indicate on a scale from 1 to 10, how lonely they think each of the videotaped people is. Since the judges in this example are now using an interval scale,

TABLE 4.1 Two Judges' Classifications of Five People as Lonely or Not Lonely

	Judge	
	I	*II*
Person		
A	L	L
B	L	NL
C	L	L
D	NL	NL
E	NL	NL

L = lonely
NL = not lonely

TABLE 4.2 Two Judges' Ratings of Loneliness of Five People on a Scale From 1 to 10.

	Judge	
	I	*II*
Person		
A	3	4
B	4	7
C	2	1
D	6	9
E	6	10

it would be appropriate to correlate their scores. The numbers in table 4.2 illustrate how the judges' ratings might look. The correlation between these ratings reaches statistical significance ($r(4) = .97$, $p < .01$) so we might conclude that our judges are consistent.

What does a researcher do when the level of agreement is not satisfactory? First, judges can be asked to discuss and, if possible, resolve their differences. If disagreement persists, it may be necessary to revise the rating scale and/or the observation procedures.

In this example we used observers to judge a person's characteristic. Another, more common approach in social psychology, is to use self-ratings. Let us imagine that we want to use a self-report measure to study loneliness. One of our first tasks is to find some way of measuring loneliness. We could, of course, just ask people if they are lonely. Some people, however, may not want to admit to being lonely. In the literature on loneliness there are several measures of loneliness and normally it would be a good idea to use one of these. For our example, however, let us design our own measure.

Imagine that we decide to make up a loneliness questionnaire with twenty questions on it. Some of the questions will be about friends, some about a spouse, and some about personal relationships (e.g., are they satisfying?). We decide to name our scale the Loneliness Across Generations Scale (LAGS).

Inter-test Reliability

One way social psychologists try to find out if a test is a reliable measure is by administering the test on two or more occasions. This procedure is used to establish what is known as **test-retest** or **inter-test reliability.** By correlating the scores on the two occasions, researchers can find out if the scores are consistent. Consistency over time is one indication that the measurements are reliable.

If we administer the LAGS to a group of people today and again in two months, we could correlate people's scores on the two occasions. This correlation would tell us the test-retest reliability.

A researcher may be concerned that people will simply recall their responses on the first test and repeat them on the second in order to appear consistent. Of course this will be less of a problem if the test-retest interval is relatively long. To avoid the problem altogether the researcher could use two forms, containing matched questions. In this case the instruments are sometimes called *parallel forms*.

Intra-test Reliability

We can also obtain an indication of the reliability of a test by seeing if people's responses are consistent across items (called **intra-test** or **internal reliability**). This is important if we want to combine the items into a total score on the test. Consider, for example, the 20 items on the LAGS. If each item on the test measures the same thing, the sum of a person's responses to the 20 items will give us a reliable score. If the items measure different things or just random error, then the total score will be meaningless.

To examine intra-test or internal reliability, we correlate one part of a questionnaire with another part of the same questionnaire. Thus, on our 20-item LAGS questionnaire we could correlate the score on items 1 to 10 with the score on items 11 to 20. This is called a *split-half procedure.* Alternatively, we could correlate the score on the odd-numbered items with that on the even-numbered items. This is called the *odd-even method.*

Yet another alternative is to use a random procedure to divide the test items into two equal sets. One problem with this procedure is that each time we carried it out, we would get a different reliability score. To avoid this problem many researchers use a measure of internal consistency called **Cronbach's alpha.** The value of Cronbach's alpha for a given test is positively related to both the average of the inter-item correlations and to the number of items on the test (Carmines & Zeller, 1979).

What if we find that our test has low reliability? One way to increase reliability is to increase the number of measurements we take. Thus, instead of merely asking a subject whether he has many friends, it might be a good idea to ask also about a spouse, about support networks, and about the nature of personal relationships. By combining the answers to these questions into one loneliness score we would be likely to get a measure that is more stable and therefore more reliable. (As we noted before, increasing the number of measures and taking an average decreases the random error.)

If the reliability of our test is still too low, we might consider the possibility that the test is measuring more than one construct. If we divide the test into subtests, each measuring something slightly different, we might find that each subtest has high internal reliability. For instance, we might find that the LAGS has separate subscales for support networks, personal relationships, and relationship to one's spouse. Responses to each of these subscales might be internally consistent but not consistent with responses to any of the other subscales.

Too often social psychologists doing research do not spend enough time searching for and developing reliable measures for their dependent variables. A newly updated book by Robinson, Shaver, and Wrightsman (1991) gives reliability information about many social psychological scales.

Validity

In earlier chapters on experimental design we addressed the concepts of internal and external validity. Internal validity has to do with whether the manipulation of the independent variable is responsible for the difference in the dependent variable. External validity has to do with whether the results of the experiment can be generalized to other subject populations, settings, treatments, etc.

Here we are considering validity from a different perspective. Is our instrument itself accurate and is it measuring what it is supposed to measure? We will refer to this validity as **test validity.**

We can divide test validity into two general types, **criterion-oriented** and **construct validity.** When there is a criterion that we accept as valid we usually choose a criterion-oriented approach to validate our test. When there is no such criterion we look for construct validity (Cronbach & Meehl, 1955).

Criterion-Oriented Validity

To estimate criterion-oriented validity we must find an outside criterion variable with which to correlate the test scores. This can sometimes be difficult. One approach is to see if we can use the score a person gets on our test to predict how the person will behave. If the criterion is future behavior, then we are using **predictive validity.**

Suppose we design a test to distinguish between good and poor car drivers. After designing the questions, we establish the reliability of the test. Now we want to establish whether or not our test is valid. Does it really allow us to distinguish good drivers from bad ones? We could administer our test to young people who are going to get their driver's licenses, and then five years later, we could check their driving records. We could correlate people's scores on our test with the number of moving traffic violations they incurred in the subsequent five years. "Moving violations" would not include parking violations as these are unlikely to reflect driving ability. Researchers might not accept the absence of traffic violations as evidence of good driving, but they would accept having a number of moving violations as evidence of poor driving.

Another way to establish criterion-oriented validity is to correlate our test with another test that already has established reliability and validity. If the correlation is high, we say the test has **concurrent validity.** To establish concurrent validity for our driver's test we could correlate scores on our test with the scores people receive from the driving examiner when they take their "real" driving test. One problem comes immediately to mind. How do we know whether the "real" driving test is valid? How was it validated? (Has anyone determined if it is even reliable? Do two examiners give similar marks?)

Construct Validity

In most cases social psychologists doing research are not concerned with criterion validity. For the interesting and relevant research questions there may not be a valid criterion. Cronbach and Meehl

(1955, p. 281) suggest: "Construct validity must be investigated whenever no criterion or universe of content is accepted as entirely adequate to define the quality to be measured."

When we designed an instrument to distinguish between good and poor drivers there was a criterion, moving traffic violations, which most researchers would be willing to accept as defining the characteristic we hoped to measure. However, much of the time when we do social psychological research we are interested in measuring and manipulating theoretical constructs such as attributions, schemas, and loneliness. With constructs such as these there is, unfortunately, little agreement among researchers about what would constitute either a defining criterion or a defining "universe of content." In these cases we might examine the relationship between the construct and some other theoretically relevant measure. If we find a significant relationship, we have validated our measure using construct validation.

To validate our loneliness scale, the LAGS, we could use construct validation. Based on previous research we might hypothesize that loneliness increases with age. We could administer the LAGS to a random sample of the population. Suppose the results supported our hypothesis that scores are higher for older people than for younger people. We would then be able to say that the LAGS had some construct validity.

What can we conclude if the results do not support our hypothesis? Should we conclude that the LAGS is not valid? Not necessarily. The rule of eliminating alternative explanations for observations is as applicable here as it is in other research situations. Perhaps the hypothesized relationship is wrong. First, loneliness may decrease as we grow older, or it may increase until middle age and then decrease. Second, the lonely may die young. This is always a possible explanation in cross-sectional studies. In both these cases the test may be valid but the hypothesized relationship may be wrong.

If we manage to eliminate the alternative explanations, we may conclude that the LAGS is not a valid test of loneliness. Alternatively, it is possible that the LAGS is a valid test for a construct other than loneliness. Thus, we may be measuring a construct other than the one we thought we were measuring—we may be confounding constructs. This is analogous to the problem of establishing the conceptual validity of the independent variable.

Summary

In general we can divide dependent measures into obtrusive and unobtrusive measures. These are also known as reactive and nonreactive measures. When a researcher uses obtrusive measures, people are aware that they are being observed, that their behavior is being studied and recorded. When a researcher uses unobtrusive measures, people are not aware that they are being observed. Using unobtrusive measures avoids the threat of reactivity but raises the ethical problem of invasion of privacy.

The problems associated with the dependent measure are the problems associated with measurement in general, i.e., reliability and validity. A reliable instrument is one that gives repeatable measures. It measures something besides random error. A valid instrument is one that is accurate—it measures what we want it to measure. A reliable instrument may or may not be valid, but an unreliable instrument can clearly not be valid. There are three ways commonly used to assess reliability: (1) The ratings of two or more judges may be correlated (inter-rater reliability); (2) The scores on the same test (or parallel versions of it) taken at two different times may be correlated (inter-test reliability); (3) Responses across items on the same test may be correlated (intra-test reliability).

We normally distinguish between two general ways of establishing validity. To establish criterion-oriented validity we correlate the measuring instrument with an outside criterion that is generally accepted as valid. When this is not possible we try to establish construct validity by using a theoretical construct to validate the measuring instrument.

While we have considered problems related to the measurement of the dependent variable, we have not considered actually designing a dependent measure. Issues relevant to designing one type of measure, a questionnaire, are considered in chapter 6, on survey research—measuring attitudes and opinions. Before we get to surveys we will discuss, in chapter 5, alternatives to experimental designs.

Alternatives to the Experimental Design

Nonexperimental Alternatives

Small-N Designs	Quasi-Experimental Designs
Case Studies	Nonequivalent Control Groups Design
A–B–A Designs	Separate Sample, Pretest–Posttest,
Multiple Baseline	Quasi-Experimental Design
Time Series Designs	Time Series with Control Group
	Design
	Correlational Designs

When planning a study to determine causality, the design of choice is an experiment. There are several situations, however, in which an experiment may be impossible. There may be problems manipulating the independent variable or randomly assigning subjects to conditions. Or, there may be too few subjects (or cases) available for an experiment.

The problem of too few cases frequently occurs in applied work outside the laboratory. This is a particular problem when we want to assess the effectiveness of a remedial program or treatment. For instance, the government may establish a program to deal with the problem of elder abuse in only two or three locations. Scientists may devise a treatment for a disorder from which few people suffer. Such research designs—to study the impact of an independent variable when there are few subjects—are called **small-N designs.**

In addition to the small-N problem, studies conducted outside the laboratory often suffer from lack of experimenter control. For example, authorities may select candidates for some new treatment or program on a "first-come, first-served" basis. When the independent variable involves the occurrence of some event like the election of a political party, a layoff of workers at a plant, or the passage of some legislation, it makes no sense to even talk about random assignment. People other than the experimenter decide when the event will occur and which people will be affected by it. Researchers use **quasi-experimental** and **correlational designs** to study the impact of an independent variable when people have not been randomly assigned to conditions. Quasi-experimental is the term for some nonexperimental designs used to study the impact of an independent variable when subjects cannot be randomly assigned to conditions. (Do not confuse quasi-experimental designs with quasi-control groups, used to study demand characteristics.) Correlational is the term for other nonexperimental designs using correlations to study the impact of an independent variable when subjects cannot be randomly assigned to conditions.

In this chapter we will consider small-N designs, quasi-experimental designs, and correlational designs. The distinctions among these designs, although clear enough in principle, are often blurred in practice. For example, researchers often use quasi-experimental and correlational techniques in small-N studies. We will maintain the distinctions here, however, because they will help us illustrate once again some of the threats to internal and external validity as well as some of the ways researchers can overcome these threats.

Small-*N* Designs

The term **N** is an abbreviation for "number." In experimental designs, N refers to the number of *independent* units, usually subjects, under study. Subjects, however, may not always be independent of each other.

Rowell and Dawson (1981) conducted a study to extend a teaching method from individual situations to whole classes. They tried to teach the Piagetian concept of conservation to eighth grade students (in separate classes) and evaluate the outcomes using a Solomon four-group design. Four classes were randomly assigned to treatment/no treatment and then randomly assigned to pretest/no pretest. In their analysis Rowell and Dawson treated each child in the class as an independent subject. They found that on the posttest, scores in class 1 were significantly higher than scores in classes 2, 3, and 4 (which did not differ among themselves.) On the basis of this result, they concluded that their method could be effective in classrooms, particularly when accompanied by pretest.

For our purposes, the most important problem with this study is that the children in each class are not independent subjects. That is, the behavior of one person, be it teacher or child, could affect the behavior of all of the other children in the class. It is not hard to imagine different teachers in each class (the authors do not say if four different teachers were involved) behaving differently. Even if the same teacher was used in all classes, he could have treated the classes differently. Furthermore, the children in each class presumably interacted with each other. If one child in the class grasped the concept of conservation she may have explained it to the other children in terms they could understand. Thus, differences between the classes could be due to history or maturation. The authors do not tell us if the classes were the same before the study began so differences could also be due to preexisting differences (i.e., the problem of selectivity).

One way to deal with this problem is to consider each class as an independent unit. Had they treated the classroom as the unit rather than the child in the classroom, Rowell and Dawson (1981) would have had $N = 4$.

The classroom example illustrates the situation where the researcher is faced not with a shortage of subjects but with a shortage of *independent* subjects. A similar situation arose in 1979 when the Canadian government established new family court systems in four different cities across the country. The researchers who wanted to assess the impact of the new courts had a shortage of independent units to examine. In cases like this, a small-N design is unavoidable.

In other situations, however, there may simply be too few instances of the event the researcher wants to study. Suppose a researcher wants to study the impact of social support on adults who were sexually abused as children. He may find few people willing to come forward and admit they were sexually abused as children.

Obviously, the fewest subjects or cases we can have in a study is 1. We will refer to this special case of small-N designs as ''$N = 1$ designs.'' There are several designs we can use when $N = 1$. For example, we can use two of the designs we discussed in chapter 2: the X–O design or the X–O with a control group design. Obviously, the second of these designs is preferable if a comparable control group is available. In each of these designs we make one observation, and it is taken after the event.

We can improve the internal validity of any small-N design by increasing the number of observations we make on each subject or case. Depending on the design, we may observe the same person several times or different people at different times. For example,

Newcomb (1961) studied the development of friendships among first-year college students living in a boarding house. He took weekly measures on the same students for one semester. The single case was the boarding house; the behavior of the people living there was measured many times.

Consider another example, a study of shoplifting by Ross and White (1987). They tallied the number of arrests for shoplifting in one city each month for four years. The single case was the city in which the shoplifting took place. Different people were included each month although some people may have been arrested more than once.

Case Studies

Case studies are another form of small-N design, carried out on one person or case. They are usually descriptive in nature. Because of the number of threats to the internal and external validity of the case study, it is not possible usually to make any causal statements. Whether or not this is a serious disadvantage depends on the goal of the research. If the goal of the research is exploratory or descriptive, there may be no problem doing a case study. On the other hand, a case study may not be suitable to test a causal hypothesis. However, there will be times when the researcher's choice is between a case study or no study at all.

Case studies to test hypotheses are rare in social psychology. One example is a study by Festinger, Riecken, and Schachter (1956), that tested an hypothesis derived from cognitive dissonance theory. When a group of people believe a major event, such as an earthquake, is going to occur, and it does not occur, you might think they would simply give up the belief. Festinger and colleagues predicted something quite different. They thought that people whose beliefs had been disconfirmed would try to convert others to their beliefs. By converting others, people can gain social support and convince themselves that their beliefs must be right.

Focus of the study was a group of otherwise rational people who believed that the world was going to end on a specific date. Before that date the group members made no effort to proselytize; after that date they did. The results of this case study confirmed the researchers' hypothesis and supported the theory of cognitive dissonance.

Case studies are more common in clinical psychology, neuropsychology, sociology, and anthropology. Clinical and neuropsychologists sometimes come across an unusual person (e.g., one with a rare clinical disorder or one with brain damage) and study this person in depth. Sociologists and anthropologists sometimes collect information by spending extensive time in a single community or with a single social group (see, for example, the classic study of street corner society by Whyte, 1943).

When the purpose of a case study is purely descriptive, threats to internal validity may not be problematic. On the other hand, when the researcher wants to draw conclusions about cases other than the one studied, we may question the study's external validity.

Let us take an imaginary case study and compare the problems that arise when it is used for descriptive purposes with those that arise when it is used to make a causal statement. Suppose a researcher studies the stress experienced by workers on an offshore oil rig. She finds that men working on this rig experience higher stress levels than do those working on shore. At this level the result is purely descriptive. Would it be appropriate for the researcher to generalize her results and say that there are higher levels of stress among all offshore workers? We cannot determine the external validity of this case study. For instance, we don't know how similar this rig is to other rigs. We don't know the impact of the environment in which this rig is operating. Is it the North Sea or the Gulf of Mexico?

Suppose the researcher did the study at the oil company's request because of a high number of accidents on the rig. In this case she could report that there was a high level of stress on the rig and that this might be related to the accident rate. Could she conclude that the stress caused the accidents? For one thing she must first establish time order. Did the high levels of stress cause the accidents or did the high accident rate cause the stress?

When the purpose of the case study involves making inferences about the causal impact of a single event there are several threats to internal validity. One of these is selectivity. To deal with this threat we need to have information about what the case was like before the event occurred. The next example of a small-N design provides this kind of information.

A–B–A Designs

The $A–B–A$ design is a more general form of the $O–X–O$ design we described in chapter 2. The design may use one or more pre- and postevent observations. If you increase the number of observations—e.g., $O\ O\ O\ X\ O\ O\ O$, you have a time series design. We will discuss time series designs later in this section.

BOX 5.1
An Example of a Natural *A–B–A* Design

Mrs. Holland's mother had twelve healthy children but four of
Mrs. Holland's own children have died within six hours of
being born. Although autopsies have found no medical reason
for the deaths, Mrs. Holland is convinced that radioactivity is
to blame. Her first and third husbands were exposed to
radioactivity while in the military and these husbands were
the fathers of the four infants who died. Mrs. Holland's
second husband was not exposed to radioactivity and her
child by this husband was healthy.

From Mother Jones Magazine (© November 1986), Foundation for National
Progress (p. 10).

There is an interesting example of an *A–B–A* design in box
5.1. In this case, *A* refers to husbands one and three who were exposed to radioactivity. *B* refers to husband two who had no exposure. To challenge Mrs. Holland's conclusions we must consider
what alternative explanations there could be for the death of the infants fathered by husbands one and three.

One of the threats to the internal validity of Mrs. Holland's
conclusion is the threat of history. The fact that she had a normal
child with husband number two weakens this threat. Some external
influence that caused the deaths of the infants fathered by the first
husband would have had to cease for a period and then start up
again. This is possible, but it is less likely than if the healthy baby
had been by either her first or third husband.

Maturation may also be a threat to the internal validity of
Mrs. Holland's conclusions. Were there changes in Mrs. Holland
herself that could have caused these deaths? For example, what was
the condition of Mrs. Holland's health during these marriages?
Might her health while living with the military husbands have been
poorer than when living with the nonmilitary husband? People in
the military may not earn as much as those employed outside the
military. As a result, Mrs. Holland may have had a poorer diet
while married to the military men and her poor diet could have affected the health of her infants.

If we were concerned with clarifying Mrs. Holland's case, we
could examine her financial status during these marriages. If it re-
mained unchanged, we could rule out the alternative explanation

having to do with diet. This is the essence of making causal statements based on nonexperimental designs. We try to think of alternative explanations for a set of results and then search for evidence that is relevant to these explanations.

As noted in chapter 4 on dependent measures, when you use nonreactive, unobtrusive methods people are less likely to be aware that they are being studied and less likely to react to the measurement process itself. One researcher used nonreactive measures with an *A–B–A* design and minimized the threats of instrumentation and testing. (Pleasant smell, 1992). With the cooperation of one of the hotel casinos in Las Vegas, a researcher piped pleasant smells into the area around the slot machines. He reported that during the forty-eight hours the smells were put into the air, gamblers put 45 percent more money into the machines than they had on the weekend before and the weekend after the test.

In this study instrumentation was not a threat since the system of counting the money in the machines was not changed. Testing was not a threat because the gamblers were not aware of being observed. However, history was still a threat. Perhaps particularly rich tourists were staying at the hotel that weekend.

There are more elegant examples of the *A–B–A* design than the one provided by the unfortunate Mrs. Holland or by the Las Vegas researcher. These examples involve further alternations or combinations of *A* and *B*. For instance, *A–B–A–B, A–B–B–A,* etc. By extending the sequence we reduce the threat of both history and maturation. The threats of instrumentation and testing, however, remain. We can eliminate the threat of instrumentation with carefully trained observers and well-established measures. If we use reactive measures, however, the threat of testing increases as the number of tests increases. In deciding how many reactive tests to employ, we must weigh the seriousness of the threats posed by history and maturation on the one hand, and repeated testing on the other. The alternative is to use nonreactive measures.

Multiple Baseline

We can use multiple baseline designs (MTB) whenever we have more than one subject and when we can collect information before the manipulation. Like most designs, the strength of the MTB increases with the number of cases. In these designs, the researcher gathers pretest or baseline measurements from all subjects before the manipulation. The independent variable is then introduced sequentially to one subject at a time and its impact is assessed.

TABLE 5.1 Multiple Baseline Designs

```
a. O   X   O
           O   X   O
                   O   X   O
```

```
b. O   X   O   O   O   O   O
   O   O   O   X   O   O   O
   O   O   O   O   O   X   O
```

The researcher may collect pretest measures immediately before the manipulation as in table 5.1a. We will refer to this as the
MTB(a) design. You can think of this as a repeated version of the
O–X–O design. The pretest on each subject serves as a comparison
measure for the posttest information collected from the previous
subject.

The researcher can rule out more threats to internal validity if
she can collect more than one pretest measure, as in table 5.1b. We
will refer to the design depicted here as the MTB(b) design. Both
MTB(a) and MTB(b) designs differ from true experimental designs
because there are not enough independent subjects to allow random
assignment to conditions. However, the order in which the independent variable is introduced to the subjects can, and should, be
randomized.

Let us imagine that you are a research design consultant. A
hospital administrator who wants to introduce a patient-care procedure for patients on five wards approaches you for help. The admin-
istrators want to know if the procedure will affect patient morale.
They ask you to design a study to assess the impact of the new
procedure.

Since there are only five wards you know that a small-N
design will be necessary. You recommend that they collect information about patient morale for all patients in all wards for three
months. Following that they should introduce the procedure first in
ward A, two months later in ward B, two months after that in ward
C, and so on until they have introduced it in all five wards. At the
same time they should measure the morale of patients on all five
wards. If the new procedure is beneficial, morale should improve in
each ward when it is introduced. There should be no change in morale in a ward before the procedure is implemented.

History is unlikely to be a threat in a multiple baseline study. For history to be a threat, some extraneous event would have to start and stop each time the independent variable was introduced. Whether or not maturation is a threat depends on how the order of exposure to the intervention is determined. If the subjects determine their order, maturation could account for the results.

Suppose another imaginary situation—that the hormonal changes occurring with puberty lead some teenagers to experience headaches for a few months. Suppose, further, that some of these teenagers go to an adolescent health center to be treated for their headaches. They receive treatment in the order they arrive at the center. For the first three weeks, before treatment begins, researchers collect baseline information. Since the headaches are time limited, they would disappear a few months after treatment. Thus, the apparent success of the treatment would be due to maturation. If the researchers randomly select a treatment starting time for each subject, maturation is less likely to be a threat, particularly as the number of subjects increases.

Testing is less of a threat to the internal validity of MTB(a) than MTB(b) designs. This is because there are fewer measures taken in the MTB(a) design. On the other hand, a researcher is more likely to detect the effect of testing with the MTB(b) design than they are with the MTB(a) design. If testing is having an effect, a change should be evident in the pretests in the MTB(b) design. The threat of instrumentation is the same in both designs. We can minimize it with reliable, valid measures and well-trained observers. Mortality is a particularly serious threat in small-N designs because it reduces our already small subject population.

The major threat to the external validity of multiple baseline designs is an interaction between testing and the intervention. Because of the possibility of such an interaction, there is always the question of whether or not our treatment would be effective in situations where there were no pretests. Clearly, this is not a threat if the researcher uses unobtrusive measures, as did the casino researcher in Las Vegas.

Another threat to external validity in multiple baseline designs is reactivity. In these kinds of studies the subjects are usually aware they are research participants. We cannot eliminate the threat of reactivity unless we can collect the pre- and posttests using unobtrusive observations. Such a procedure would, of course, eliminate the threat posed by testing as well.

Time Series Designs

Conceptually, *time series designs* are straightforward—a series of measures are taken over time. Although the data collection is simple, the analysis is not. We will first consider time series designs and then, briefly, time series analysis.

The reliability and the analysis of time series designs depend on the number of observations. The more observations we make, the more reliable the measure. The number of observations depends, in turn, upon the length of the study and the interval between observations. A researcher could make one observation a minute for one hour or for two hours. In the first design there would be 60 observations, in the second, 120. On the other hand, an observer who makes one observation a month for five years also would have 60 observations. It is up to the researcher to define the appropriate interval between observations or measures.

In 1984, a newspaper started publishing the names of people who had been convicted of drunk driving or shoplifting. Ross and White (1987) in an $N = 1$ study, used a time series design to analyze changes in the rates of drunk driving and shoplifting. Using police records they examined the number of arrests for these two offenses for three years before and eighteen months after the newspaper started publishing names. The effect on shoplifting can be seen in figure 5.1. Ross and White found that arrests for shoplifting went down after the newspaper started publishing names. (Publishing the names had no effect on the number of people arrested for drunk driving.)

Did shoplifting become less frequent because the newspaper published shoplifters' names? To answer this question we need to look at the threats to the internal validity of this design. When we are looking at a case rather than an individual person, it is particularly difficult to distinguish between history and maturation. However, as we said earlier, our objective is to find alternative explanations for the results, not to label them. We seek alternative explanations without being excessively concerned about whether the alternative explanation is history or maturation.

One alternative explanation for the results of the shoplifting study has to do with the behavior of people other than the shoplifters. It is possible that store owners and police became more reluctant to charge a person with shoplifting because they knew the person's name would appear in the newspaper. Nothing in the police

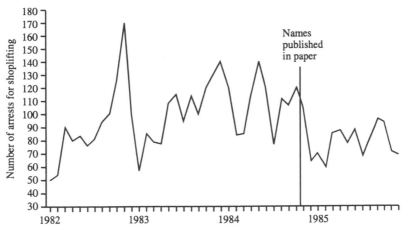

FIGURE 5.1
Time series design—Shoplifting offenses between January 1982 and
December 1985.
From Ross, A. S. & White, S. (1987). Shoplifting, Impaired Driving and Refusing the
Breathalyzer: On Seeing One's Name in a Public Place. In *Evaluation Review,* 11 (No. 2),
254–260. Copyright © 1987, Sage Publications. Reprinted with permission of Sage
Publications.

records allowed the investigators to discount this kind of explanation. However, interviews with store owners and police officers
might have been helpful in this regard.

Did other events occur that could account for the change in
shoplifting frequency? Such events would have to have occurred at
the time the newspaper policy came into effect. If they had occurred
a few months before or a few months after the newspaper initiated
the policy, their impact would have been seen as an earlier or later
change in the number of arrests. It is possible, however, that the
local police started a program for store owners, aimed at reducing
shoplifting, around the same time the newspaper started publishing
names. Thus, in this study we cannot completely eliminate history.

Historical coincidence is more likely to be a factor if a policy
has been implemented in reaction to an extreme condition. Suppose
that shoplifting had been unusually prevalent in 1983. It is possible
that steps to deal with this problem might be taken by several agen-
cies at the same time. This introduces another threat to internal validity, **reactive interventions** (Kratochwill, 1978).

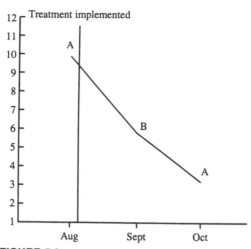

FIGURE 5.2
A–B–A design to assess effectiveness of treatment.

Sometimes interventions are undertaken in response to some extreme situation (e.g., an unusually high number of road deaths, an extremely painful headache, or an unusually high incidence of shoplifting). If the extreme situation is simply a temporary fluctuation caused by chance factors, the intervention will appear to be successful when conditions soon return to normal. Conversely, an intervention that occurs when matters are proceeding unusually smoothly may be unfairly blamed for making things worse. Reactive intervention is less likely to be a problem in situations where the researcher controls the time at which the intervention is applied.

In figure 5.2 there is an example of how a reactive intervention might appear in an *A–B–A* design. In figure 5.3 we can see the same intervention but viewed as part of a time series. An extreme swing in the variable the researcher is studying occurred in August. In response, steps were taken to deal with the extreme situation. Imagine a study with an *A–B–A* design that used data from August and September. The researchers would conclude that the intervention was successful. However, had a longer term study been underway, with observations extending backward and forward in time, the researchers would be able to see the extreme swing and the return to the average.

There are several ways to measure change when examining time series data. The methods range from the simple to the sophisticated. If the impact of the intervention is very strong and the background variation small, statistical tests may not be necessary. (In this case

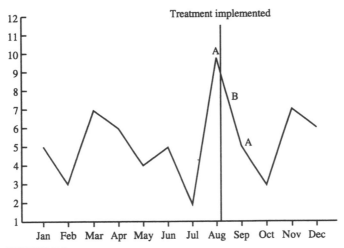

FIGURE 5.3
A–B–A as segment of time series design.

we rely on the famous "eyeball test.") Unfortunately, the results are not so clear cut in most social psychological studies. In such cases, statistical methods are necessary and the more observations, the better. When there are at least 50 observations, the method most often suggested by statisticians is ARIMA (*Auto Regression Integrated Moving Averages*) analysis. When there are fewer than 50 observations, there is less consensus among statisticians about the most appropriate method of analysis. A further discussion of time series analysis is beyond the scope of this book.

Quasi-Experimental Designs

As we have said in previous chapters, when investigating causality, the experiment is the design of choice because it has the strongest internal validity. In many situations outside the laboratory, however, it is not possible to assign subjects randomly to conditions. For example, people may already be separated into work shifts or classrooms. When random assignment is not possible, we cannot carry out a true experiment. Instead, we resort to quasi-experimental designs.

In many respects, quasi-experimental designs resemble designs already considered in this chapter. The essence of the quasi-experimental design, however, lies in the various control groups we include to eliminate alternative explanations. In most cases these alternative explanations arise from the researcher's inability to assign people to conditions randomly. Consider the following example.

An insurance company decides to computerize the head office to increase efficiency. They hire an applied social psychologist to assess the impact. She immediately faces the problem that computers are being given to everyone in the operation. Individuals and starting times cannot be randomly determined. Therefore, she needs a quasi-experimental design.

One way she can assess changes is by measuring efficiency before and after the company introduces the computers. This is the standard *A–B–A* design we discussed in the section on small-*N* designs. As we saw, history, maturation, testing, and instrumentation threaten the internal validity of this design.

Quasi-experimental designs are essentially a patchwork. That is, for each alternative explanation for the results that she can think of, the researcher must find a control group (or groups) that will help eliminate this explanation.

Nonequivalent Control Groups Design

In the insurance company computerization example, the psychologist might be wise to look for another insurance company to serve as a control (see table 5.2). She must find another company as similar as possible to the one being studied. Since she cannot find one that is identical, she must concentrate on similarity of relevant characteristics. Consider three characteristics: location, company size, and gender of employees. Suppose the researcher cannot find a match on all three characteristics. Perhaps she thinks company size and employee's gender are more likely to affect reactions to the computers. She would then look for another company of the same size with a similar ratio of male and female employees. On the other hand, if she does not think that geographic location will affect employees' reactions to the computers, she will not limit her search for a comparison company to the same city or state.

If the psychologist were to measure efficiency in the control company before and after the computers were introduced in the experimental company, she could eliminate several threats to internal validity. She could eliminate history because external changes should affect workers in both companies. Similarly, testing and instrumentation factors would be the same for both companies. However, she could not eliminate maturation. One of the control companies might also make changes. This could provide an alternative explanation for the results. By adding more control companies we can reduce the threat caused by changes in the control companies. It would be unlikely that all comparison companies would also make internal changes.

	Pretest	Manipulation	Posttest
TABLE 5.2 Nonequivalent Control Groups Design. (People are not randomly assigned to groups A and B.)			
Group A	X	X	X
Group B	X		X

Consider a situation where people put themselves into one of the two groups. Suppose a government department introduces a television campaign to encourage women to breast-feed their children. Researchers measure women's attitudes before and after the campaign. At the time of the posttest, the researchers ask the women if they saw the television messages. Those who say they did see them comprise group A; those who say they did not see them comprise group B.

This design is susceptible to the threat of selectivity. It is possible that women who were already favorable to the idea of breast-feeding were more likely to notice the advertisement. If so, we would expect to find differences in the pretest attitudes of the two groups. If the researchers find pretest differences, they cannot rule out selectivity.

Even if there are no pretest differences, in any pretest design with reactive measures, the possibility of an interaction between testing and the intervention poses a threat to external validity. The pretest might make the women aware that the researchers are studying their attitudes. The questions asked might lead them to think about issues they would otherwise ignore. This, in turn, might affect their reactions to the advertising campaign. If this happened, the results could not be generalized to a population that had not been pretested.

Separate Sample, Pretest–Posttest, Quasi-Experimental Design

This design avoids the problem of an interaction between testing and the intervention (see table 5.3). As the name suggests, different samples are measured for the pretest and the posttest.

The researchers could have used this design for the breast-feeding study we described earlier. They could have measured the attitudes of one sample of women before the campaign and those of

TABLE 5.3 Separate Sample, Pretest/Posttest Design.
(People are not randomly assigned to
groups *A* and *B*.)

	Pretest	Manipulation	Posttest
Group A	X	(X)	
Group B		X	X

a different sample after the campaign. Because they measure each woman's attitudes only once, the effect of the pretest on reactions to the advertising campaign would not influence the posttest scores.

Proper random sampling and assignment are imperative for the separate-sample design to succeed. There must be no chance for bias in deciding who is measured before and who is measured after the campaign. This design has very good external validity but is vulnerable to the threats of history, maturation, and mortality.

Time Series with Control Group Design

This is the final quasi-experimental design we will consider. Earlier we pointed out that history is the major threat to the internal validity of the time series design, but by using an appropriately selected control group we can minimize this threat. As an example, consider the situation where a company hires an applied social psychologist to find out the impact of a change in routine on the work attitudes of people on a production line. Let us expand that example into a time series design.

The social psychologist knows that the company will make production changes in July. He collects weekly measures of work attitudes from January to December. He finds that work attitudes improve after the company introduces the production change. Is it appropriate to conclude that the change in attitudes is due to the change in work routine?

There are at least two ways that history could play a role in this situation. First, other changes in the company could have occurred also. It is possible that everyone received a bonus in July. Second, history could have affected the results through normal seasonal swings or variation. Perhaps everyone's work attitude improved in July because summer vacations were near. The researcher could assess the possibility of seasonal variations by collecting information about work attitudes from a production line in the company where there was no change in routine. If he found no change in attitudes in this section, he could eliminate history as an alternative explanation for the results.

Another threat to the time series with control group design is testing. People's work attitudes and even their productivity may change as a result of the testing procedure itself. An early illustration of this phenomenon was a study carried out between 1927 and 1932 and described by Homans (1965). A company separated six women, who worked at producing telephone relays, from the rest of their coworkers. It assigned them to work together in a room where the company manipulated various environmental factors. Changes in the work place, especially changes imposed by management, are usually assumed to contribute to stress. To the surprise of the researchers, virtually every alteration in the working conditions resulted in an *increase* in the productivity of these workers.

Part of the reason for the increased productivity of the experimental group seemed to be that the six women became a very cohesive, social group. They interacted with each other both on and off the job and they covered for each other by working extra hard when one of their group was not feeling well. The other reason for the increased productivity seemed to be that the workers got the feeling that the six of them were special (although, in fact, the company selected them because they were average), that the company was concerned about their welfare and was interested in doing something to improve working conditions. The tendency for workers to work especially hard when they feel they are part of something new and special is known as the **Hawthorne effect** after the name of the plant where these women worked.

One way to minimize the kind of threat to validity posed by the Hawthorne effect is to combine the time series design with a separate sample pretest–posttest design. Instead of measuring work attitudes of the same workers each month, the researcher could draw a random sample from both production lines each month.

Perhaps you can think of more alternative explanations for a change in work attitudes. The task for the researcher who uses a quasi-experimental design is to think of as many alternative explanations as possible. The researcher must then think of ways of collecting the data needed to minimize or rule out these alternative explanations.

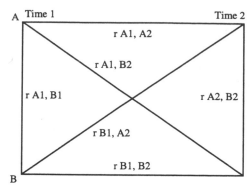

FIGURE 5.4
Cross-lagged correlation.

Correlational Designs

Normally, conclusions about causality cannot be drawn from a correlational study. If we find that two variables are correlated we have shown concomitant variation but we have not established time order nor have we ruled out alternative explanations for the results. A cross-lagged correlation design enables us to draw some conclusions about causality, in part, by helping us to establish the time order.

A cross-lagged design involves collecting data on two variables, *A* (the hypothesized causal variable) and *B* (the hypothesized dependent variable), at two separate times (1 and 2). The six possible pairwise correlations are then computed (see figure 5.4). Correlations between variable *A*, measured at one time, and variable *B*, measured at a different time, are called cross-lagged correlations. In figure 5.4 the correlation between *A1* and *B2* is the forward, cross-lagged correlation and the correlation between *A2* and *B1* is the backward cross-lagged correlation.

If factor *A* is indeed the causal variable, then we would expect the forward, cross-lagged correlation to be significant. Since *A1* came before *B2*, the time order is consistent with our hypothesis. However, for the backward, cross-lagged correlation, the time order is inconsistent with our hypothesis. So, *A2* could not possibly have caused *B1*. Therefore, if the hypothesis that *A* causes *B* is correct, the backward, cross-lagged correlation should not be significant.

A thorough analysis of cross-lagged designs involves comparisons among the six possible correlations, not just the forward and backward, cross-lagged ones. Detailed discussions of the analytic

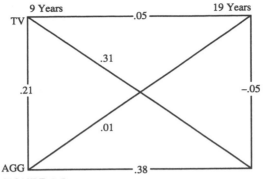

FIGURE 5.5
Cross-lagged correlations.
From Eron, L. D., Huesman, L. R., Lefkowitz, M. H., &
Walder, L. O. (1972). "Does Television Violence Cause
Aggression?" in *American Psychologist, 27* (No. 4), 253–263.
Copyright © 1972 by the American Psychological
Association. Reprinted by permission.

procedures that are appropriate with this kind of design are beyond the scope of this book. We will end the present section with a brief description of a study that used the cross-lagged procedure to draw conclusions about the effect of viewing violent television programs on aggressive behavior.

Eron and colleagues (1972) retested adolescents they had originally tested as children 10 years earlier. In 1960 they measured aggression and television viewing on 875 children who were in third grade (approximately 9 years old). Then in 1970 they obtained similar measures on 427 of the same children. The first time they measured viewing by asking mothers to name their children's three favorite programs and having judges categorize the programs for violence. The second time they asked the adolescents for their favorite programs. Aggression was measured at both times by peer ratings.

The correlations between the variables can be seen in figure 5.5. Had this study ended after the first phase when the children were young, the researchers would have been unable to distinguish between two alternative explanations for the results. They would have been unable to tell if watching violent television led to aggressive behavior or if aggressive children were more likely to watch violent television programs. By adding a second phase to their study and measuring the variables ten years later, they obtained the cross-lagged correlations.

Eron and colleagues' interpretation of their results is too complicated to go into in depth. However, two findings stand out. The forward cross-lagged correlation between the violence of television programs watched at age 9 and aggressive behavior at age 19 ($r = .31$) was stronger than either (a) the backward, cross-lagged correlation between aggressive behavior at age 9 and viewing violent television at age 19 ($r = .01$) or (b) the correlation between television watching and aggression when both measures were taken at age 9 ($r = .21$).

The results led the researchers to hypothesize that there was a critical period in which watching violent programs on television led to aggressive behavior. There is, of course, one major threat to the results of this study, mortality. The researchers' first observations were on 875 children. Ten years later they only managed to contact 427 of the original group. One way to assess the impact of mortality is to examine the initial scores (Time 1) of the people who could not be contacted later (Time 2). When Eron and colleagues did this they found (p. 255):

> The dropout rate from participation in the study between the third and thirteenth grade was considerably higher for subjects who displayed high aggression in the third grade than for those who displayed low aggression.

Unfortunately, the authors did not discuss the implications of this finding for the validity of their conclusions.

Summary

When it is not possible to randomly assign subjects to experimental conditions a researcher must search for alternatives to experimental designs. When there are not enough independent subjects, small-N designs can be used. Case studies are carried out on one person or case, and are usually descriptive in nature. A–B–A designs involve observations before and after a treatment. Multiple baseline designs require that the treatment be introduced sequentially to subjects and that the researcher collect information before and after the treatment is introduced. Time series designs require multiple observations both before and after the treatment is introduced.

When there is no shortage of independent subjects but they cannot be randomly assigned to conditions, researchers can use quasi-experimental designs and correlational designs. With quasi-experimental designs the researcher must anticipate threats to internal and external validity. Information must then be collected from appropriate control groups to rule out these threats. By collecting correlational information at two different times, a cross-lagged correlation allows a researcher to draw conclusions about causality. It does this, in part, by allowing the researcher to eliminate time order as an alternative explanation for the results.

All of the alternatives that we have discussed in this chapter are susceptible to threats to internal and external validity. Hence, if the researcher has a choice, preference should be given to a true experimental design.

With this chapter we finish our consideration of designs where we are trying to establish causality. In the next chapter we start discussing surveys which are usually used in descriptive research.

Surveys—Measuring Attitudes or Opinions of a Population

CHAPTER

Measuring Attitudes or Opinions

Questionnaires
    Question Content
    Question Type
Systematic Bias
    Social Desirability Bias
    Interviewer Bias
    Wording Bias

Random Error
    Question Wording
    Faulty Memory
    Lack of Knowledge

Almost everyone in North America is familiar with surveys. A survey is usually conducted to describe a population at a particular time. You can think of it as a snapshot of people's attitudes or opinions. We will just talk here about attitudes or opinions. However, a survey can measure almost any characteristic in a population, such as health condition, physical characteristics, income, etc. Everything we say about attitudes or opinions is true for any survey regardless of its objective.

For example, a survey reported in the newspaper found that in 1985, 73 percent of the population were satisfied with their personal economic situation. Although this was a static snapshot, we can gain more information by comparing it to other snapshots, taken at other times. The same newspaper reported that in 1984 the surveyors found that 76 percent of the population were satisfied with their personal economic situation. Taken together, these percentages appear to indicate that people were less satisfied in 1985 than they were a year earlier, although the statistical significance of the difference would need to be tested.

Within the static snapshot we may also be able to explore the relationships among people's attitudes and to compare attitudes of people in different segments of the population. For instance, we might find that people who are in favor of capital punishment also believe that sparing the rod spoils the child (corporal punishment) and that both attitudes are more common among older persons than among younger ones.

Surveyors concerned with assessing the proportion of people in a population who hold an attitude or opinion want an **absolute measure** of a population. Exactly how many people, or what proportion of the population believe in corporal punishment for children? On the other hand, in research we often want to know if people in one group hold opinions that are different from those of people in another group. For instance, if we found that older persons were more likely than younger ones to favor corporal punishment, we would have a measure of the difference between attitudes in two subpopulations. This would be a **relative measure.** That is, we are describing one subpopulation relative to another. In this chapter we will be discussing absolute measures.

We cannot usually make causal statements on the basis of a survey. Sometimes survey researchers will manipulate the order or wording of questions to investigate the impact on answers—which could be considered a true experiment. However, this involves investigating the survey form itself rather than describing the population. Given the snapshot nature of a survey we can conclude only that two variables are correlated. Usually we can not be sure of the time order; nor can we eliminate alternative explanations for the results.

A national survey of Canadians conducted in May and June, 1992 found that almost half of the people interviewed said they felt "really stressed" either all the time or several times each week. About 60 percent said that work and financial worries were the leading cause of their stress and depression. The survey results (Recession-induced funk, 1992) led the president of the Canadian Psychiatric Association to conclude that, ". . . difficult economic times facing [Canada] are clearly having a significant negative impact on the mental health of Canadians."

Is this a valid conclusion based on the results of this survey? We can probably eliminate time order as an explanation for the results. It is not likely that people's stress and depression caused the recession. (However, some economists have argued that lack of consumer confidence leads to lack of spending and that this may extend a recession.) What alternative explanations are there for this result? We do not know how people felt about their jobs one, two, or ten years ago. Perhaps people feel "really stressed" and worried about their work in times of economic expansion as well as during a recession. Since we only have this one time "snapshot" we cannot eliminate this alternative explanation.

Another problem with using a survey to assess causality can be seen in a study by Wolf, Kissling, and Burgess (1986). These researchers were interested in examining the changes in life-style of medical students. In a two-month period they surveyed freshmen, sophomores, juniors, and seniors in medical school. They found that compared to freshmen and juniors, seniors exercised vigorously more frequently, slept more hours per night, and consumed less caffeine. They also found that freshmen spent more time studying. Based on these findings they concluded that the senior year in medical school was not as stressful as the previous three years.

Another explanation is possible: (a) the time order is reversed, and (b) this factor, combined with the threat of mortality, could account for the results. Perhaps exercise helps a student cope with the stresses of medical school. Students who don't exercise have trouble coping with medical school and drop out before they reach the last year. The students who reach the senior year may have exercised more vigorously and frequently than their peers throughout their medical training. Had the researchers taken measurements at more than one time, they might have been able to eliminate this alternative explanation (or to find that it accounted for their results).

The objective of a survey usually is not to assess causality, but to measure the attitudes or opinions of a population at a point in time. In the remainder of this chapter we will consider how attitudes and opinions are measured in various types of surveys. In the following two chapters, we will examine how samples are drawn from a population and how surveys are administered to the people in the sample.

To understand how surveys measure population characteristics, it is important to recall from our earlier discussion of measurement (chapter 4) that the score we assign to a person on a dependent variable can be viewed as a combination of a true score, systematic bias, and random error. In a survey the true score is the value of some population characteristic (for example, the average amount of beef eaten in a week or the percent favoring a particular position). Systematic biasing factors present in the measurement process will consistently elevate or depress people's scores, regardless of their true scores. Finally, random error factors in the measurement process will cause scores to fluctuate over time, independent of variability in true scores.

In our discussion of surveys we will first consider the measuring instruments used. We will then consider sources of systematic bias, and finally, sources of random error.

Questionnaires

In most surveys, the measuring instrument is the **questionnaire.** Whether administered orally or in written form, the building blocks of the questionnaire are queries or questions demanding a response. In formulating questionnaires, researchers need to consider both *content* and *type* of questions included.

Question Content

The questions on a questionnaire are usually of three kinds: those that ask about **demographics,** those that ask about **behavior,** and those that ask about **psychological states.**

Questions about Demographics
Demographic information covers topics such as age, sex, marital status, employment status, and occupation. Demographic questions are important for comparing how different groups of people (e.g., men and women) respond to questions. The questions can also provide a useful check on how similar the people interviewed are to the rest of the population. For example, if a sample from the general population contained only 30 percent females, we would certainly question whether our results can be generalized to the population at large.

Questions about Behavior
Questions about behavior ask about actions a person took or plans to take. The answers to such questions are often verifiable. If a person says she went to Niagara Falls last weekend, we can check to see if she did. If a person says he plans to attend church next Sunday, we can check to see if he does.

Questions about behavior can sometimes be threatening—a source of embarrassment regardless of the response. The person may be reluctant to admit to exhibiting the behavior (if it is socially undesirable) or to avoiding it (if it is socially desirable.) Admitting that you have been charged with sexual harassment could be embarrassing. At the same time, admitting that you have not given money to a worthwhile charity may also be embarrassing (obviously, not to the same degree).

Questions about Psychological States

Questions about psychological states ask about a person's attitudes or opinions. The answers to such questions are not easily verified unless the attitudes or opinions are clearly linked to specific actions. For example, a person may express support for women. If the person later attends a demonstration in favor of equal rights for women this might be considered verification of the belief in equality. However, if the person does *not* attend the demonstration, the implications for the underlying belief are less clear. There may be many situational reasons for not attending a demonstration that have nothing to do with support for equal rights.

Question Type

The questions a researcher asks about demographics, behavior, or psychological states may be either **closed-ended** or **open-ended.** The difference between these two types is that closed-ended questions present response alternatives while open-ended questions do not. You are familiar with one type of closed-ended question, the multiple choice question, beloved by all who make up examinations. Open-ended questions allow respondents to use their own words in answering the question. The most familiar type of open-ended question is the essay question on examinations.

Closed-ended Questions

The alternatives presented with a closed-ended question can take several forms. A person may be asked to choose among alternative actions. For instance:

If an election were held tomorrow would you vote for the

a. Liberal Party?
b. Conservative Party?
c. undecided?

Factual knowledge can also be quickly and easily assessed using this type of question.

> How many days into the term may a student drop a course without an academic penalty?
>
> a. 5?
> b. 10?
> c. 15?

Another common type of closed-ended question asks a respondent to express agreement or disagreement with a statement. For instance:

> Abraham Lincoln was the greatest U.S. president.
>
> 1. Agree strongly
> 2. Agree moderately
> 3. Neither agree nor disagree
> 4. Disagree moderately
> 5. Disagree strongly.

Open-ended Questions

Qualitative questions do not constrain the answers that a respondent can give. For example, we could ask:

> Who do you think has been the greatest U.S. president?

If a researcher were trying to find out what people think of Abraham Lincoln, either the closed-ended or open-ended version of this question could be used. The closed-ended question would indicate the average rating respondents give Abraham Lincoln. The open-ended question would indicate how many respondents spontaneously name Abraham Lincoln as the greatest president. The format used will depend on the type of information needed.

In the open-ended Abraham Lincoln question, a person would respond with one name. Further open-ended questions could be used to elicit more information:

> *Why* do you think [the person you have named] was the greatest president?

Responses to this question would tell us what variables people consider when evaluating a president's performance.

Closed- or Open-ended Questions?

Each question form has advantages and disadvantages. Closed-ended questions are quick and easy to score. However, they may be more difficult to compose and may not yield as much information as open-ended questions. The alternatives presented in a closed-ended question may not be relevant or meaningful for some respondents. For example, a question asking about political party preference (Democratic, Republican, or Don't know) might pose a problem for a person who prefers a fringe party or one who has decided not to vote in order to protest the poor quality of the candidates. Extending the list of alternatives can lessen the problem, as can adding a final alternative, "Other." However, we may still fail to include all alternatives, and some people may be reluctant to use the "Other" category.

The advantages and disadvantages of open-ended questions are the opposite of those for closed-ended questions. Open-ended questions allow for rich data. The answers can yield information that might be missed with closed-ended questions. For instance, Connidis (1983) asked a sample of people 65 years or older in an Ontario community:

> If circumstances were to change and you had to choose between living with a child or in a facility for seniors, which would you prefer?

She found (p. 363) an "overwhelming tendency to choose a facility for seniors rather than living with children."

Connidis then asked respondents why they felt this way. Answers to the qualitative question were coded according to their dominant theme—either positive (a reason *for* an option) or negative (a reason *against* an option). For example, one person who chose the facility for seniors said, "I would like to be with people my own age." This answer was coded as a positive reason for choosing a seniors' facility. Another person who also chose the facility for seniors said that living with children was ". . . not fair to the children." This was coded as a negative reason for choosing a seniors' facility. Of course, many people gave more than one reason. Connidis then had to develop a method of coding to deal with these cases.

Answers to the open-ended question showed that the preferences for the seniors' facility were mainly based on negative factors. The majority of respondents who preferred the seniors' facility phrased their reasons in terms of not wanting to live with their children. They were concerned that they might become a burden on them. In contrast, the majority of the respondents who said they preferred to live with their children gave positive reasons—e.g., "I'd rather live with a child if circumstances permitted, for comfort and companionship."

By asking the open-ended question, Connidis was able to clarify her results. Had she just asked the first question, she might have concluded that most elderly people want to live in seniors' residences. Responses to the *why*-question allowed her to interpret these responses as avoidance rather than attraction.

A disadvantage of open-ended questions is that they may be difficult to analyze. The very richness of the responses makes scoring difficult. General categories of answers must be established either a prior or after examination of the data. Then a scoring key must be devised. Finally, scorers have to be trained and inter-rater reliability established. As you can imagine, this is time consuming and can be expensive.

Systematic Bias

Systematic bias can arise from the desire of the respondents to appear in a favorable light (**social desirability bias**), from cues in the situation where the questionnaire is administered (**interviewer or context bias**), and from the way in which questions are worded (**wording bias**). We will consider each of these sources of bias in connection with questionnaires that seek information about demographics, behavior, and psychological states.

Social Desirability Bias

In answering some kinds of questions, people may be strongly influenced by a desire to look good. For instance, most people want to respond positively to the question, ''Did you give money to a charity last year?'' Reliance on answers to a question such as this would likely cause us to overestimate the true frequency of charitable donations in the population.

In some cases, an answer may be seen as socially desirable by a member of a subgroup, but not by everyone in the population. Consider the question, ''How many bottles of beer did you drink this past weekend?'' If the respondent is a teenager, upward distortion may occur. If the respondent is an adult, the distortion may be in the opposite direction.

Interviewer Bias

Systematic bias can be induced by the characteristics or the behavior of the person asking the questions. If an interviewer were dressed as a clergyman, it might affect responses to questions about church attendance. If the interviewer appeared to be a police officer, it might affect the hypothetical teenager's response to the question about amount of beer consumed.

The interviewer's verbal and nonverbal behavior may convey to a respondent what the "best" answer is. Interviewer bias has not been studied as much as experimenter bias. However, most interviewers are told not to respond positively or negatively to a person's opinions. It is not hard to imagine how a person's responses would be affected by an interviewer who nodded and said, "Good" or "I agree" every time a particular opinion was expressed.

Open-ended questions are particularly susceptible to interviewer bias. Because it is difficult to record every word a person says, summaries are necessary and any summary may reflect a conscious or unconscious bias on the part of the person making it. Tape recording answers may lessen the problem or it may only postpone having to deal with it. At some point the respondent's answers to open-ended questions must be interpreted.

Wording Bias

Earlier we distinguished among questions about demographic characteristics, questions about behavior, and questions about psychological states. Questions in each of these categories are susceptible to systematic bias. We will discuss each area in turn.

Demographic Questions

Questions about a person's background may appear to be simple and straightforward, but there are pitfalls to avoid. For example, let us look at the problem of ascertaining a person's age. A straightforward question such as, "How old are you?" might lead to bias because some people may not want to give their true age. In a society where youth is valued, older people may report being younger than they are. Conversely, adolescents may report being older than they are if the questionnaire deals with topics such as drinking, voting, or driving. Nowadays, many airlines, hotels, and banks give seniors reduced rates. This might lead to a counter pressure for those approaching the age of 60 to over-estimate their age.

Similarly, many people are threatened by questions about income. This cannot be attributed to embarrassment about poverty because it seems to hold true across all income levels. Researchers need to become sensitized to the kinds of topics that would elicit such a response.

TABLE 6.1	Age Decades to be used to Determine Respondent's Age
	<19
	20–29
	30–39
	40–49
	50–59
	60–69
	70–79
	80–89
	90 or older

When we suspect that people may distort the truth, it may be a good idea to give them a list of categories and ask them to indicate the group to which they belong. Such a procedure may appear to be less of an invasion of privacy. Instead of asking people how old they are, they can be given a list of age decades (see table 6.1) and be asked to indicate their own. This procedure might lessen distortion, but it creates another potential problem. At some point in our research we might want to compare our sample to a regional or national one. Table 6.2 lists the age categories that are sometimes used in reporting the Canadian Census. Because the groupings in table 6.2 are different from those reported in table 6.1, it would be virtually impossible to make an exact comparison of the age distributions.

A different way to avoid distortions in age reporting is to ask people for their birth date. Most people who distort their age have not recalculated a corresponding birth date. Also, birth dates allow you to construct any age categories you want for subsequent comparisons.

We have gone into detail on the problem of age reporting in order to illustrate some of the difficulties that can arise in obtaining what appears to be simple information. Whenever you design a demographic question (or indeed any question) it is a good idea to see how it is asked in the appropriate census. The people who design census surveys have spent a great deal of time formulating and refining demographic questions. A good source for the wording of demographic questions is the *Basic Background Items for U.S. Household Surveys* published by the Social Science Research Council (1975). In Canada, census questions are available from Statistics Canada in the *Social Concepts Directory* (1980).

TABLE 6.2	Age Decades Sometimes Used by Statistics Canada to Report Age Distribution

0–14
15–24
25–34
35–44
45–54
55–64
65–74
75–84
85 or older

Questions about Behavior

As discussed earlier in the chapter, questions about behavior can sometimes be threatening—thus inviting distorted responses. Designing such questions thus requires some ingenuity. A number of techniques have been developed for asking threatening questions. Some less than serious examples may be seen in box 6.1. In our opinion it is better to leave threatening questions to the end of the questionnaire.

Questions about Psychological States

Questions about attitudes or opinions may give rise to systematic bias if they are worded in such a way that respondents do not feel they can disagree (or agree). For example, consider the statement, "Wilderness areas must be preserved for our children." How could a person disagree with preserving something for future generations?

The two following statements appear to be biased in opposite directions: "The government should provide support for those who are unfortunate enough to be unemployed" and "Those who are too lazy to work should not receive government support." The biasing word in the first statement is "unfortunate"; in the second, it is "lazy."

If the wording of a question communicates our expectations to the respondent, it is also biased. "How much would you be willing to pay to ride on the Toronto subway?" This question conveys the expectation that the respondent is willing to pay something. This may not be true. One study in the 1960s which we've heard about, found that people were willing to "pay" –$.50 to ride on the Chicago subway. That is, the people running the subway would have to pay the riders fifty cents to ride on it!

BOX 6.1

A young man lends his father his car for the evening. The next morning the son discovers a dent in the front fender. He wants to find out how the dent got there without antagonizing his father. He decides not to ask his father the direct (but threatening) question, "How did you put the dent in my car?" He can choose from several survey alternatives.

The Causal Approach: *Oh, by the way, did you happen to put that dent in the car?*

The Numbered Card: *Would you please read off the number on this card which corresponds to what happened to the car?* (Hands card to father.)

1. I ran into a wall.
2. A wall ran into me.
3. I ran into another car.
4. Another car ran into me.
5. Other (What?)

The Everybody Approach: *As you know, many people have been putting dents in cars recently. Did you happen to put a dent in any cars?*

The "Other People" Approach:

a. *Do you know anyone who has put a dent in a car recently?*
b. *How about yourself?*

Ask the question at the end of the questionnaire, or just before the father leaves to go shopping.

Adapted from Barton, A. J. (1958). Asking the embarrassing question, in *Public Opinion Quarterly, 22* (pp. 67–68). Copyright © 1958, The University of Chicago Press. Reprinted with permission of The University of Chicago Press.

Biased wording is often difficult to detect because the perception of bias may depend on one's attitudes. A person designing a questionnaire for a nature group might not see any bias in the statement, "Wilderness areas must be preserved for our children." However, a person whose salary depends on a job with a logging company might think it biased. On the other hand, such a person

BOX 6.2
Using a Survey to Design a Referendum Question

Before the 1992 Canadian referendum on the Constitution, the federal government used surveys to test the wording of the question to be voted on. The final wording of the question was, "Do you agree that the Constitution of Canada should be renewed on the basis of the agreement reached on Aug. 28, 1992?" Most people agreed that the wording chosen would bias people toward a "Yes" vote. Informed sources said that various drafts of the question were tested night after night in a tracking survey before the final wording of the question was decided upon.

might see no bias in the statement, "Feeding a family is more important than preserving trees." Somehow, items which favor one's own side seem fairer and more neutral!

There are times when a surveyor may be less concerned with biased wording. One of these is when we want to make relative rather than absolute statements about a population. Suppose we want to compare upper and lower class people's attitudes toward support for the unemployed. As long as the question is equally biased for both groups, we can make comparative statements. Take the statement, "The government should provide support for those who are unfortunate enough to be unemployed." Based on responses, we could still say that upper socioeconomic status (SES) people are less sympathetic to government support for the unemployed than are lower SES people. If we used a statement biased in the opposite direction (e.g., "Those who are too lazy to work should not receive government support"), we should still end up with the same relative result. However, in neither case could we say what percent of the population actually is in favor of government support for the unemployed.

There are times when a group prefers a biased question. Many of us receive what appear to be surveys in the mail (often accompanied by a request for funds). Their purpose is usually advocacy rather than the accurate determination of opinions in a population. These cannot be considered properly objective surveys. An interesting example of a survey being used intentionally to select biased wording can be seen in box 6.2.

Although we have concentrated on the wording of the questions, the wording or order of the alternatives presented to the respondent may also cause bias. Mean and colleagues (1989) asked respondents to evaluate their overall health. Respondents were asked, "Would you describe your health as . . . ?" Half the respondents selected a response from the following list: excellent, very good, good, fair, or poor. The other half of the respondents selected a response from the same list but in a reverse order: poor, fair, good, very good, or excellent. The researchers found that respondents who saw the excellent-to-poor list rated their health more positively than did respondents who saw the poor-to-excellent list. Merely reversing the order of alternatives affected people's responses!

Random Error

As we have said before, random error factors influence different individuals in the population in different ways. Many factors can contribute to random error. Some of these factors will be unknown to researchers; others will be apparent but beyond control. In this section we will consider some factors that might contribute to random error, but that can often be controlled.

Question Wording

Some types of questions or statements should be avoided. For example, **complex questions** that contain difficult words, negatives, and double negatives will often confuse respondents and render their answers meaningless. Suppose we asked university professors to agree or disagree with the following statement:

> Teaching assistants should not be allowed to grade nonobjective examinations.

What does it mean to disagree with this negative statement? It probably means that assistants *should* be allowed to grade essay examinations. It might, however, take respondents a while to work through the double negative (even if they were university professors) and the potential for error would be high.

Another type of wording that can cause problems occurs in statements with more than one complete thought (**double-barrelled statements**). For example, a person might be asked to indicate agreement or disagreement with the following statement:

> University admission standards should be raised to reduce overcrowding.

There are really several distinct issues here. Should admissions standards be raised? Is there overcrowding? Is raising the standards the best way to reduce overcrowding? A person might agree that there is overcrowding but not think that raising standards is the best way to reduce it (perhaps more classrooms should be built and more teachers hired). Would such a person agree or disagree with the statement? Another person might think that too much class time is spent explaining basic material to weak students. This person would agree that admission standards are too low and should be raised. However, the reason for agreement in this case is not to reduce overcrowding but to use class time more efficiently. How should this person respond to the statement?

Questions that can be answered in the same way for different reasons are referred to as **nonmonotonic questions.** They are not double-barrelled because they ask only one question. Consider a person who is asked to agree or disagree with the following statement:

> Only material showing nudity should be censored.

If the person agrees with the statement, the attitude is clear. But there are at least two very different reasons why a person might disagree with this statement. The person might disagree, thinking that nothing should be censored or that everything should be censored.

Faulty Memory

Faulty memory can sometimes inflate random error in people's answers to questions about their behavior. For example, Mean and colleagues (1989) interviewed people who belonged to a university health plan. They asked them about visits to the health center in the previous year and compared their answers to their medical records.

They found that people recalled only 41 percent of their health-plan visits. To analyze the results further, the researchers divided health events into recurring events (conditions that had led to three or more visits in the past 12 months) and nonrecurring events. Thirty-two percent of the respondents recalled recurring health events, while fifty-three percent recalled nonrecurring events.

The researchers found that people have problems remembering visits to a physician in the previous 12 months. The events they do recall tend to be the unique ones; things that did not occur frequently. Imagine the problems respondents would have remembering events that took place years ago, particularly if we were asking about events that occurred regularly.

Lack of Knowledge

Respondents' lack of knowledge can be a serious source of random error in their answers to questions about their psychological states. The question the Canadian government decided to use in the referendum (box 6.2) was: "Do you agree that the Constitution of Canada should be renewed on the basis of the agreement reached on Aug. 28, 1992?" Some people may not know exactly what was in the agreement reached on August 28th, but be unwilling to ask for fear of appearing uninformed. As a result, their votes may be based more on incorrect assumptions than on the content of the agreement.

The topic of a question, or of an entire survey, may not have much relevance or importance for some respondents. Whatever topic you consider, there will be some people who do not have any real attitude toward it. Without an attitude to guide their responses, people may respond to such questions with on-the-spot judgements that are particularly susceptible to situational cues. Faced with the same questions the next day, their responses might well be quite different. This can lead to a high degree of random error in the results. We call this the problem of **nonattitudes.**

There are several ways of dealing with the problem of nonattitudes. One of the simplest is to include, "don't know," "no opinion," or "undecided" in the response options. One problem with this method, however, is that conscientious respondents may feel they are not being very helpful if they repeatedly choose what appear to be uninformative alternatives.

A better solution to the nonattitude problem is to begin the survey with some questions about the importance of the topic. Has the respondent thought about the topic, discussed it with friends, read about it in the newspaper, or heard it discussed on radio or television? Questions of fact also help to find out whether the respondent is likely to have formed an attitude on a topic.

Summary

When we design a questionnaire we need to consider question content and question type. Question content can be divided into questions about demographics, behavior, and psychological states. Demographic questions ask about things like age, sex, or occupation. Questions about behavior ask about actions a person took or plans to take. Depending on the behavior of interest, the answers to these questions may be threatening or embarrassing. Questions about psychological states ask about a person's attitudes or opinions.

There are two general types of questions, open- and closed-ended questions. Closed-ended questions present response alternatives from which the respondent can choose, while open-ended questions do not. Closed-ended questions are quick and easy to score. However, they may be more difficult to compose and may not yield as much information as open-ended questions. Open-ended questions allow for rich data. The answers can yield information that might be missed with closed-ended questions. However, the analysis process can be complex.

When designing questions we try to minimize systematic bias. Systematic bias can arise from the desire of respondents to appear in a favorable light (social desirability bias), from cues in the situation when the questionnaire is administered (interviewer or context bias), and from the way in which questions are worded (wording bias).

At the same time we try to minimize systematic error when designing questions, we also need to minimize random error. Random error factors influence different individuals in the population in different ways and may be influenced by the wording of the question, the respondent's memory, and the respondent's lack of knowledge. Complex questions, double-barrelled questions, and nonmonotonic questions are wording hazards that may contribute to random error. Not remembering a past event or not having any knowledge of the topic being surveyed can also contribute to random error.

When you read the results of an attitude survey you should consider all of the issues we have discussed in this chapter. You should look for information about how the researcher dealt with each problem. In the absence of such information, a degree of skepticism about the results is warranted.

In this chapter we have considered how to design a questionnaire. In the chapter that follows we will consider how to select a sample of respondents and how to administer the questionnaire.

Administering the Questionnaire

In the previous chapter we discussed the measurement of attitudes or opinions. We used a measurement model to consider different aspects of measurement. Our purpose now is to discuss the population that is being assessed. We will continue to use the measurement model as a way to conceptualize the process of describing the population.

When social scientists want to describe the characteristics of the people in a population, they use survey procedures, usually in conjunction with some form of population sampling. The idea behind sampling is a simple one—the characteristics of the people sampled should resemble the characteristics of all the people who *could have been sampled.*

Although the concept of sampling is simple, implementing the procedures may be a complex process. A sample that contains characteristics distributed similarly to those in the population from which it is drawn is said to be a **representative sample.** A description of a representative sample can provide a basis for inferring the characteristics of the population from which it was drawn. A sample that does not resemble the characteristics of all of the people who could have been sampled is said to be a **biased sample.** A biased sample cannot provide a basis for inferring the characteristics of the population from which it was drawn. Representative samples are sometimes extremely difficult to obtain.

Using the measurement model, we can think of a characteristic of the population as the true score. The characteristic of the sample (analogous to the observed score) is a function of the population value (true score) and sampling error. Sampling error may be the result of systematic bias or random error or both. When we look for systematic bias in a sample, we are searching for a consistent difference between the sample and the general population. Proper sampling techniques minimize the chance of systematic bias.

While statistical tests allow us to evaluate the effect of random error, they do not tell us about systematic error. Our purpose in this chapter will be to describe some of the problems associated with different sampling techniques and the dangers of relying on some of the more frequently used shortcuts.

We will begin by distinguishing between survey sampling and some other techniques that are sometimes used to describe populations. In some cases the population may be sufficiently small or the resources of the person seeking the information may be sufficiently extensive that all members of a population may be contacted and questioned. The result is a *census.* For example, a professor may ask each member of a class to indicate a preference for one of two different dates for an examination. A census may be especially useful on sensitive issues where, for the sake of later unity, it is important that each member of the population feel that his or her position has been taken into account. In addition, in a census, there is no need for concern about the representativeness of the people questioned, no need for techniques of statistical inference, and of course, no sampling error. These are major advantages but the cost of conducting a census is often prohibitive.

Another technique to describe a population, favored more by social and political activists than by researchers, is the *petition.* In a petition, members of a population are asked to sign their names in support of a statement on one side of some social policy issue. The number of people who are willing to do so is taken as a measure of support in the population for the position expressed in the petition.

From a scientific point of view, the number of names on a petition might be informative if we knew about the sources of sampling error. How did the person gathering the names select people to approach? How many of the people who were approached refused to sign? Answers to these questions would tell us about sources of systematic bias in those signing the petition. Such information, however, is rarely, if ever, made available.

Another technique that, like the petition, is often closely associated with the political process, is the *referendum* or *plebiscite*. Members of a population are encouraged to express an opinion either for or against a proposed law or policy. For example, Canadians may be asked whether or not Quebec should remain part of Canada and Danes may be asked whether or not Denmark should join the European Economic Community. If the referendum is conducted by government, all the machinery of elections (e.g., voter registration, polling stations, ballot boxes, and scrutineers) together with full-scale campaigns by different interest groups may come into play. Less formal kinds of referenda are often conducted by the hosts of radio call-in shows and by the editors of newspapers and magazines.

Unlike a petition, in the case of a referendum there is usually at least a pretense of impartiality by the people posing the questions. In addition, in a referendum, the numbers of votes for all of the response alternatives are announced at the conclusion. The major problem with the referendum, however, is that respondents select themselves; they decide whether or not they want to vote. Self-selection of voters in a referendum may be a source of both systematic bias and random error. People who vote in a referendum may not be representative of the total population. In general, it seems likely that people who vote in a referendum will have stronger opinions than those who do not.

A survey sample differs from a referendum in that, in a survey sample, the researcher selects the respondents who will take part. In this respect, the sample survey is similar to the petition. However, the person conducting a petition attempts to recruit all those in the population with a particular point of view. The person selecting the survey sample uses a system of selection whereby he or she has no control over which individuals are selected. Following the sampling procedure means that individuals will be selected regardless of their views. Using a proper system of selection minimizes systematic bias and should yield a sample representative of the entire population. In this chapter we will examine some of the different ways in which samples may be obtained.

Sampling from a Population

A single member of a population is called an **element.** It is important to note that the elements of a population are not always individual persons. In some cases, for example, the population elements might be the living units or residences in a city. In other cases, families, work groups, neighborhoods, or schools might constitute the population elements.

It is possible to distinguish between **probability** and **nonprobability** samples. Probability samples are also known as **random** samples, nonprobability as **nonrandom** samples. Further distinctions within each of these categories are shown below.

- a. Nonprobability samples
    - i. Accidental
    - ii. Purposive
- b. Probability samples
    - i. Simple random
    - ii. Stratified
    - iii. Multi-stage

We will first discuss the differences between probability and nonprobability samples and then the different subtypes.

In a probability sample, all elements of a population have a specifiable probability (usually an equal probability) of being included. A probability sample, if properly executed, should minimize systematic error and yield a representative sample. In a nonprobability sample there is no way of estimating the probability of any element being selected. A nonprobability sample is likely to be a biased one.

Suppose a professor with a large class of 500 students wants to determine how many students think she lectures too quickly. A class list and a table of random numbers might be used to obtain a probability sample of students to interview. If done properly, every student in the class would have an equal probability (i.e., 1/500) of being sampled.

In a nonprobability sampling procedure, the professor might stand outside the classroom before class and ask the fifty students who arrive first if her lectures are delivered too quickly. With this procedure it is impossible to estimate the probability that any particular student in the class will be included in the sample. In addition, it is easy to imagine many ways in which students who arrive for class early might differ from those who arrive later.

The next sections examine these two general categories of sampling in more detail. We will first discuss nonprobability samples and examine their flaws. We will then discuss probability samples and problems of sample bias.

Nonprobability Samples

When one considers the disadvantages of nonprobability sampling, it is reasonable to wonder why anyone would choose such a procedure. There are at least two reasons. First, there are times when the researcher is not concerned about a representative sample. Second, a nonprobability sampling procedure is often convenient and appears to be economical. We will consider each of these factors in connection with the two kinds of nonprobability samples, **accidental** and **purposive samples.**

Accidental Samples

An interviewer who surveys the first or most easily contacted elements of a population is using an accidental sample. Accidental samples are used in the person-in-the-street interviews that you see in the newspaper or on television. A passerby is stopped by a reporter and asked his or her opinion on some topic of national or local interest.

The validity of an accidental sample is suspect because of the potential for systematic bias. For instance, the people in a shopping mall on a particular afternoon are not likely to be representative of the rest of the population. They are likely to be predominantly female, not employed outside the home, and middle or upper class.

An accidental sample is convenient, but whether or not it is economical will depend on the purpose for which it was gathered. A news editor may simply want to get a number of different points of view expressed in the everyday language of the street. Such expressions almost always have considerable entertainment value and may be used to lighten an otherwise deadly serious discussion of the issues. Nonprobability samples are well suited for this purpose and any extra money, time, or effort spent on obtaining a probability sample would likely be wasted. On the other hand, if one wants an accurate picture of the population, then the effort, however small, of obtaining a nonprobability sample has been wasted.

Although the problems are obvious, some surveyors who use accidental samples claim that their results have predictive validity. For example, prior to national elections in the U.S., a movie theater manager in a large city has two kinds of popcorn boxes available for his patrons. One box has a picture of a donkey for the Democrats

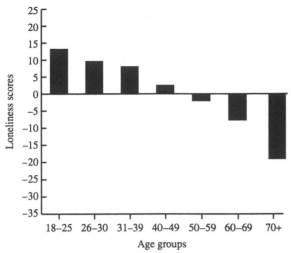

FIGURE 7.1
Loneliness scores in different age groups responding to a
newspaper survey. An example of the results of an
accidental sample.
Based on Rubinstein, C., Shaver, P., & Peplau, L. A. (1979).

and the other has a picture of an elephant for the Republicans.
Moviegoers who purchase popcorn can request one box or the other.
The manager claims that his patrons' box preferences closely pre-
dict the results of the national election!

Accidental samples have occasionally been used by serious researchers. For example, Rubenstein, Shaver, and Peplau (1979) published a questionnaire in the Sunday section of several East Coast
newspapers in the Spring of 1978. More than 25,000 people responded! The researchers found that loneliness decreased with age
(see figure 7.1). They also tried to counter criticisms about the possible unrepresentative nature of their sample (p. 61).

> Although newspaper surveys are subject to the bias of people who
> choose to fill out the questionnaire, we believe that the results are
> valid and representative of most of the population. Regardless of city
> size and location (for example, small town or metropolis, northern or
> southern city), the findings within each sample remained virtually the
> same. And although a few people noted that ''only a lonely person
> would bother to fill this out,'' we received thousands of question-
> naires from people who said they were not lonely. Only 15 percent
> of those who replied said they felt lonely most or all of the time, and
> only 6 percent said they never felt lonely. The majority, as one
> would expect, felt lonely on occasion.

Despite such assertions, it was still an accidental sample—hence, we may still suspect systematic bias in the sample. There may be some consistent differences between responders and the rest of the population for which the researchers did not test.

Purposive Samples

An interviewer who uses purposive sampling intentionally selects the most interesting or informative elements of the population. Sometimes, particularly in the exploratory stages of research, one wants to speak to experts who can provide guidance on a topic. For example, Ross and Grant (1982) used a purposive sample when planning an evaluation of a new family court system. One goal of the new court system was to reduce the time that people with problems had to spend at the court and to make that time less painful for them. Another objective was to reduce the problems that women experienced in collecting maintenance and child support payments from their spouses or ex-spouses. In the planning stages of the project, Ross and Grant wanted to anticipate problems that clients might have with the court.

Before the court was established, Ross and Grant selected a purposive sample of lawyers who had extensive family-law experience and were known for their outspoken views on the subject. A second purposive sample was selected that included women who were active in and had spoken publicly on women's issues. In interviews, respondents in these samples were asked open-ended questions about problems that a court with the proposed format might create. Ross and Grant used the results of these surveys to assist them in developing the questionnaires that were used in the eventual study.

Purposive samples are frequently used by sociologists and anthropologists when they conduct field research. For example, in studying a small town, a researcher might try to identify and then interview the community leaders. The researcher might also obtain useful information by attending town meetings, even though the people in attendance might not be representative of the entire town population. In a similar manner, an anthropologist might find out a great deal about the history and lore of a particular village by speaking to the elders of the village. It would not be necessary to ensure that every elder in the village had an equal chance of being selected for the interview.

There will almost always be difficulties in drawing firm conclusions from purposive samples. The accuracy of the conclusions will depend on the researcher's ability to select the best informants (that is, to avoid systematic bias) and to interpret the information they provide. Because of the subjective nature of such judgments, we believe that purposive samples are best used only in the preliminary or exploratory phases of a research project. When one wants to draw firm and quantifiable conclusions about the general characteristics of a population, it is safest to rely on probability samples.

Probability Samples

There are several types of probability (*random*) sampling techniques available to researchers: simple, stratified, multi-stage, and random-digit dialing.

Simple random samples

To design successful probability samples, a researcher needs to understand how to take what is called a **simple random sample.** In random sampling, random numbers from a table or a computer program are used to select the sample from a complete list of the elements in the population. This list is known as the **sampling frame** and constructing it is often difficult.

The problem of finding a complete sampling frame increases with the size of the population. If you wanted to conduct a survey at your college or university you could probably get a complete student list from the registrar's office. A survey of the adult residents of a city might pose a greater problem. People are often surprised to discover that in most cities there is no complete list of residents. Constructing the sampling frame for a national survey would be even more difficult. A further problem with any population list but particularly with large ones is that the information needed to contact the people on the list (e.g., phone number or postal address) quickly becomes out of date.

The potential for systematic bias exists if any segment of the population is omitted from the sampling frame. A poll taken by the magazine *Liberty Digest* in 1938 is a classic example of this problem. The results of the poll indicated that in the upcoming presidential election, Landon would beat Roosevelt by a large majority. In fact, Roosevelt won the election by a margin of 25 percent.

There are many reasons for the inaccuracy of the *Liberty Digest* poll. The reason of most interest to us concerns the sampling frame which was constructed using the telephone directory and automobile registrations. Both of these listings contained a preponderance of adult males who were middle and upper class. Female voters as well as lower class males were under-represented in the poll and it was these voters who eventually gave Roosevelt his victory.

TABLE 7.1 Population of Canada Age/Gender Characteristics, 1986

Age Group	Males	Females
15–24	11%	10%
25–44	20%	21%
45–64	12%	12%
65+	6%	8%
Total	49%	51%

Even when a sampling frame is complete, systematic bias may be introduced at any stage of the survey process. For instance, inexperienced pollsters sometimes drop people from their sample if they cannot be easily reached. You can probably think of segments of the population that are likely to be more difficult to reach (e.g., those who change residence frequently, those who are employed outside the home, or those who are in the hospital). By omitting these people you may be biasing the sample.

Stratified Random Sample
A researcher may wish to control the degree to which different segments of the population are represented in the sample. A procedure called **stratified random sampling** makes this kind of control possible. In this procedure, the researcher first divides the population into subgroups or *strata* and then draws a random sample from each of the subgroups.

Consider a researcher who wants to determine if there is a relationship between loneliness and age. The researcher suspects that males become lonelier as they age, but that this is less true of females. To test this hypothesis, the researcher administers a loneliness measure (remember the LAGS?) to a random sample of the population.

To compare levels of loneliness across different age groups, a minimum number of respondents (say, 100 males and 100 females) in each group are needed. Table 7.1 shows the percent of males and females in Canada, who are in different age groups. The number in each cell is the percent of the total population. This means that if the researcher were to draw a random sample of 100 people from the population, there would likely be 12 males between 45 and 64. In a simple random sample of 100 people, approximately 14 persons (6 males and 8 females) would be over 65.

In order to get 100 males over 65 in a simple random sample, the researcher would have to draw a total sample of almost 1,700 people. One way to reduce the required sample size would be to stratify the population by age and then randomly select respondents from within each age stratum. If the researcher did this she would need a sample of only 800 people (100 males and 100 females in each age group).

The data from a stratified random sample can be used to make several comparisons. The loneliness scores of men can be compared with those of women. The loneliness scores of young people can be compared with those of their elders. And finally, the relationship between loneliness scores and age can be compared in males and females. Do males get lonelier than females as they grow old?

It would not be appropriate, however, to use the results of the stratified random sample to draw conclusions about population averages because some groups are disproportionately represented in the sample. Older males and females are **over-represented** in the sample and middle-age people are **under-represented.** By over-represented we mean there are more older people in the sample than we would expect based on their percentage in the population. By under-represented we mean there are fewer middle-aged people than we would expect based on their percentage in the population. If older people tend to be less lonely than younger ones, as Rubenstein and colleagues found in 1979 (see figure 7.1), then the average loneliness score in the sample will be an underestimate of the average loneliness score in the general population. Unbiased estimates of population values can be obtained from stratified samples by simply weighting the mean of each stratum in the sample by the size of that stratum in the population.

In sum, stratified random samples are efficient and useful when we want to be sure we have enough members of a particular group in our sample. However, because group sizes in the sample are not proportional to group sizes in the population, sample averages must be weighted in order to estimate population averages.

Multi-stage Random Sample

When a population is very large, the problem of obtaining a complete list of its elements can be reduced by randomly sampling in successive stages—a **multi-stage random sample.** Suppose a researcher wants to know how people in the United States feel about environmental issues. The researcher might begin by drawing a simple random sample of states from the total of fifty. Next, from each of

TABLE 7.2 Population of U.S. Age Characteristics, 1975

Age	Percent
18–24	18
25–39	27
40–54	26
55–64	14
65–69	5
70–79	7
80 and over	3

From Harris, Louis, and Associates, Inc. (1975), *The myth and reality of aging in America,* Washington, D.C.: The National Council on the Aging. Copyright © 1975 by and reprinted with permission of The National Council on the Aging, Inc., 409 Third Street SW, Washington DC 20024.

the states selected in the first stage, a random sample of towns and cities would be selected. Then, for each of the towns and cities selected in the second stage, a random sample of residences would be drawn. Finally, a rule would be formulated that would enable the interviewer to select the person to interview in the residence. The main advantage of this multi-stage procedure is that at each stage, the list from which the sample is drawn is readily available and easily managed.

Multi-stage sampling can be combined with a stratified random sampling technique. For example, if environmental attitudes are expected to be different in different regions of the United States, it might be advisable, in the first stage of sampling, to randomly select states from each region (e.g., the Northeast, South, Midwest, or Southwest). Of course, if regions were sampled without regard to their differing populations, then it would be necessary to use weighted means to describe attitudes in the country as a whole.

Harris and associates (1975) conducted a survey of a nationwide random sample of people in the U.S. to look at several issues related to aging. They wanted a wide cross section of the population with an adequate representation of older people. Table 7.2 shows the proportion of people in different age groups in the U.S. at that time.

Harris and associates used multi-stage stratified random sampling. They stratified by geographic region (East, Midwest, South and West), and by size of community within geographic region. They then selected four national samples of 100 locations each (total of 400 locations). In one of the four samples they selected 21 households in each of the 100 locations (2100 households). They then randomly selected one person over 18 years of age from all those living in each household. For the other three samples they randomly selected households but interviewed a person in the household only if he or she was over 65.

Random-digit Dialing

When persons in a sample are contacted by telephone, it is possible to use random-digit dialing to eliminate the need for a complete sampling frame. In this method, a computer is programmed to generate random sets of seven digits (in some countries this may be six). If the digits correspond to an actual telephone number, the appropriate person in the household at that number—e.g., the female or male head-of-household, can be interviewed. Sets of digits that do not correspond to actual telephone numbers, so-called *false numbers,* can simply be discarded. The main advantage of random-digit dialing is that every telephone in the region has an equal probability of being called. In the case of random sampling from the telephone book, people with unlisted numbers, recently changed numbers, and newly installed telephones are eliminated.

The main disadvantage of random-digit dialing is that many false numbers will be generated for every real number. This problem can be reduced by combining random-digit dialing with a stratified sampling procedure. The strata in this case are the three-digit prefixes of phone numbers in the region where the sampling is being done. Within each of these strata, random sets of four digits can be generated. The number of sets that are generated for the different prefixes should be proportional to the population living in the exchange area.

If the area to be surveyed were a large one, random-digit dialing might be combined with multi-stage sampling. At stage one, area codes would be selected from a list or randomly generated. At the second stage, three-digit prefixes would be sampled from a list or randomly generated. Finally, in the third stage, four-digit codes would be randomly generated and appended to the digits selected in the earlier stages.

Sample Size

Sampling procedures affect systematic bias; sample size affects random error. How large a sample should be selected? This is a question that students frequently ask. First we will consider a theoretical answer to the question and then some practical factors that need to be taken into account.

The theoretical answer to the question of sample size involves what statisticians refer to as the *sampling distribution.* Assume that you have a population from which you repeatedly draw independent random samples of size *n.* Each time you draw a sample you calculate the mean and record it. The means, of course, would not all be the same. There would be some variability and you would end up with what is called a *sampling distribution of means.* Regardless of the size of the samples, the mean of the sampling distribution would be an unbiased estimate of the population mean. However, the variance of the sampling distribution (σ_m^2) would depend on the size of the samples you were drawing (*n*) as well as on the population variance (σ_p^2). As you can see in equation (1), for a given population variance, the larger the sample size, the smaller would be the variance of the sampling distribution of means (σ_m^2). This is why, in estimating a population mean on the basis of a single sample, our confidence will be greater if the sample is a large one. In statistics this is sometimes referred to as the law of large numbers (Hays & Winkler, 1970, p. 285): "The larger the sample size, the more probable it is that the sample mean comes arbitrarily close to the population mean."

$$\sigma_m^2 = \frac{\sigma_p^2}{n} \tag{1}$$

But how close is close enough? To determine the sample size needed to estimate the population mean with a particular level of confidence, you need to know or be able to estimate the population variance. With this information, a **confidence interval** can be drawn around the sample mean. The true population value is most likely to be somewhere between the upper and lower values in the confidence interval. One can calculate, for example, a value *c* so that there is a 95 percent probability that the interval defined by the sample mean ± *c* includes the true population mean. The larger the sample size, the smaller the confidence interval will be.

A simple example may help to clarify how a decision about sample size might be made in a real research situation. A researcher wants to be able to estimate the average loneliness score (on a test such as the LAGS) in some population. Scores on the test can range from 1 to 100. For our example, let us assume we know that the variance of the scores in the population is 100. The researcher wants to draw a sample from the population and to be able to say, with 95 percent confidence, that the sample mean is within five points of the population mean (that is, $c = 5$). How large should the sample be?

From equation (1) we know that the variance of the sampling distribution will be $100/n$. Thus the standard deviation (σ_m), sometimes called the standard error of the mean, will be the square root of $100/n$. In a normal distribution, we know that approximately 95 percent of the scores fall within 2 standard deviations of the mean. Thus the confidence interval that the researcher would draw around the sample mean would be equal to $2\sigma_m$. In general, if the x-percent confidence interval is defined as the sample mean $\pm c$, then the value c can be calculated by equation (2) where Z_{crit} is the two-tailed Z value associated with the $100 - X$ alpha level. To find the sample size needed to give a confidence interval of $\pm c$, we can simply solve for n in equation (2).

$$c = Z_{crit} \sqrt{\sigma_p^2 / n} \qquad (2)$$

In the case of the researcher who wants to estimate the mean loneliness score in the population, equation (3) enables us to calculate that a sample of 16 persons would have to be randomly selected from the population. If the mean loneliness score of these 16 individuals was 30, the researcher could say with 95 percent confidence that the interval between 25 and 35 contained the population mean. What if we wanted a narrower confidence interval? Say, for instance, that we wanted to be able to say that the interval between 27.5 and 32.5 contained the population mean (that is, $c = 2.5$). Again using equation (3) you can see that we would need a sample of 64 individuals. A general rule is illustrated here: to double the precision of our estimate we have to increase our sample size by a factor of four. In other words, cutting the confidence interval in half can be costly.

$$n = \frac{Z_{crit}^2 \sigma_p^2}{c^2} \qquad (3)$$

One problem with the theoretical approach to determining the required sample size is that the researcher must either know or be able to estimate the population variance. Sometimes information about population variance is available either from the researcher's earlier work or from the published work of others who have used the same measuring instrument. If the measuring instrument is a new one, then it may be necessary to collect some preliminary data, simply for the purpose of estimating the population variance. There are, however, a number of factors that can complicate the matter.

In addressing the question of sample size, Hedges (1990, p. 3) said:

> In theory, the sample size is determined by the required level of precision, the variability inherent in the relevant variable, the likely design effects of the sample design selected. . . . In principle, if you can specify all these numerically, the sample size needed can be calculated. In practice, it is not so simple. The researcher usually does not know enough about the variability of the relevant variable, and even less about the design effect. It is unusual for anyone to specify in advance the necessary level of precision. In practice, sample sizes tend to be determined by available resources, and by the requirements of subgroup analysis.

Hedges is probably correct in asserting that practical considerations are usually the decisive factors. "Available resources" means how much time and money the researcher has. "Subgroup analysis" refers to the issues we raised in the section on stratified random sampling. For instance, what sample size does one need in order to be sure that the sample will include at least 20 males over 70 years old?

Professional survey companies, such as Gallup or Decima, can accurately estimate the population variance because they have conducted many surveys. They can estimate accurately how big a sample they need for a state or a country. These survey companies charge their clients enough so that they can obtain the sample size needed in the time allowed. Most other researchers who want to conduct a survey get as many people as they can in the time they have for the money they have. Then they use the sample variance to estimate the population variance and construct confidence intervals.

The intricacies of sample size and bias can lead to problems in understanding and communicating the results of surveys. It is interesting to compare how issues related to sample size are understood by researchers and nonresearchers.

The first point people sometimes have trouble with is that the sample size needed for a survey is not linearly related to the size of the population from which it is drawn. Equation (3) enables us to estimate sample size for various confidence intervals. This equation is appropriate when the population size (N) is greater than 100,000 (Rea & Parker, 1992). When the population is smaller, equation (3) must be modified:

$$n = \left(\frac{Z_{crit}^2 \sigma_p^2}{c^2}\right) \cdot \left(\frac{N - n}{N}\right)$$

$$= \frac{Z_{crit}^2 \sigma_p^2}{c^2 + \dfrac{Z_{crit}^2 \sigma_p^2}{N}}$$

Suppose we want our estimate of some population characteristic to be within 5 points of the true value 95 percent of the time. In figure 7.2 we see the required sample size as a function of population size when the population variance is 100. As you can see, when the population is greater than 100,000 the required sample size increases very slowly with increases in population size.

The second point to remember is that, if the sample is not representative, it doesn't matter how large the sample is—it will still be biased. As an example, let us consider a survey conducted by a large professional survey company in Canada. For several decades many women in North America have received silicone breast implants. Several years later some women started having problems with them. Silicone breast implants were then banned in the United States; in Canada they were not.

The Canadian government commissioned a survey company to determine the feelings of women who had the implants. If a large percentage of the women felt they were unsafe, the government intended to ban them. Government policy would be based on the results of the survey.

It was estimated that approximately 150,000 women had the implants, but there was no list and therefore no sampling frame. To get around this problem, the researchers put advertisements in newspapers across Canada asking women who had silicone breast implants to call them on a toll-free telephone line. Approximately 3000 women responded to the survey.

Women who wanted the implants outlawed called the survey a "dismal failure." They said (*Breast Implant Survey*, 1992),

> The figures are not enough to determine whether a Canadian moratorium on the sale of the implants should be lifted.

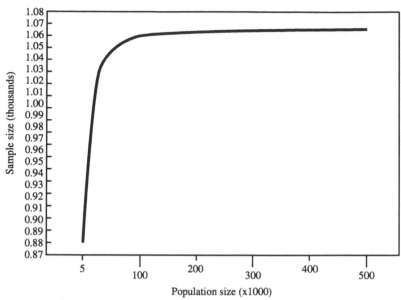

FIGURE 7.2

Sample sizes required for a 95% confidence interval of ± 5 for different population sizes ($\sigma_p^2 = 100$).

The survey company disagreed and said that the number of people who responded was adequate. A company vice-president maintained (*Breast Implant Survey*, 1992):

> . . . [the survey] attracted twice as many respondents as most national surveys. "There's certainly enough data there to make conclusions as to the opinions of the Canadian population. . . ."

Who was right? The survey company was right about the number, but the women were right to be skeptical about the results of the survey. With regard to the numbers, you can see from figure 7.2, that for a 95 percent confidence interval of ±5 points (with a population variance of 100) a survey would need only 1,068 people.

Despite the more than adequate sample size, the women were correct that conclusions could not be drawn. There is a major difference between most national surveys and the implant survey. Most national surveys use random sampling and the surveyors select the sample. In the implant survey, the surveyors had a self-selected sample. It is impossible to judge how representative such a sample is and increasing its size will not reduce the bias.

The other problem in understanding and communicating survey results stems from people's tendency to grasp and retain the unusual or salient. On one occasion known to the authors, the John Howard Society tried to establish a neighborhood halfway house for ex-offenders. Not surprisingly, several of the potential neighbors were against it. The executive director of the Society suspected that the most vociferous neighbors were not representative of all the people living in the neighborhood. He asked three social psychologists (Grant and Ross were two of them) to conduct a survey of the neighborhood. They found that he was correct; most people in the area were either in favor of the halfway house or didn't care.

The John Howard Society presented the survey results at a public meeting of the city council. At that meeting one of the outspoken neighbors presented a petition against the halfway house. She introduced it by saying, ''Well, they may have the numbers but we have the names.'' She was arguing that the concreteness and vividness of her information should outweigh the comparatively pallid survey results. And indeed, she may have been successful; the city council voted not to allow the halfway house in the neighborhood.

Alternative ways of Administering the Questionnaire

In this section we will consider how questionnaires are administered to respondents. At the same time the researcher is designing a questionnaire, she must be thinking about how the questions will be asked of the respondents. Should she mail the questionnaires to respondents and ask them to complete them and mail them back? Should she administer the questions over the telephone? Or, should she have interviewers call on the respondents and ask the questions in person?

How the surveyor administers the questionnaire depends partly on the nature of the questions to be asked. At the same time, the nature of the questions will be shaped by how the researcher plans to administer the questionnaire. In this section we will consider the advantages and disadvantages of each of the methods of delivery. After discussing each of the methods, we will consider some combinations that can be used.

Mail Survey

The main advantages of **mail surveys** are cost and anonymity; the main disadvantages are response rate and anonymity. (Yes, an advantage can also be a disadvantage.)

A mail survey is the least expensive method of asking questions. The main cost is postage to and from the respondents. (Most mail surveys include a return envelope with a stamp or prepaid postage.) A second advantage of the mail survey is the respondent's perceived anonymity. Most mail surveys do not ask for a respondent's name, address, or telephone number. With such anonymity, a person is more likely to respond honestly, particularly to threatening or embarrassing questions. Responses may be less influenced by social desirability.

One of the major disadvantages of the mail survey is the low **response rate.** Response rate refers to the number of questionnaires that are completed and returned compared to the number that are sent out. If researcher A sends out 750 questionnaires and gets back 500 the response rate is 66 percent. If researcher B sends out 200 questionnaires and gets back 200 the response rate is 100 percent. Researcher A has 300 more questionnaires than researcher B, but researcher B has a higher response rate.

Surveyors want to get the highest possible response rate. If you have a low response rate, it is likely that you have a biased sample. By this we mean that the people returning the questionnaires are not representative of the population of interest. (This is true even if the original sample was properly selected.) For instance, a number of years ago, researchers who were interested in sexual harassment on a university campus mailed out questionnaires to 9000 female undergraduate and graduate students. Three thousand questionnaires were returned and 60 percent of the women reported being sexually harassed in the previous year.

What conclusions can we draw from this survey? Can we say that 60 percent of the women on the campus were sexually harassed in the last year? No, because we don't know anything about the 6000 women who failed to respond. This is the problem with a low response rate. We know nothing about those who didn't return the questionnaire. On the other hand, we can say that at this campus, at least 1800 women reported being sexually harassed in the last year.

We stated earlier that respondent anonymity is both an advantage and a disadvantage of the mail survey. Anonymity is a disadvantage because we cannot tell who in a household filled out the questionnaire. The surveyor might want the questionnaire to be filled out by the female head of the household. However, it could have been filled out by anyone in the house (see box 7.1). People who are not literate might have others fill out the questionnaire for them or they might just throw it away (reducing the response rate).

BOX 7.1
Are You Really Certain Who Filled Out That Questionnaire?

A woman was surprised to receive a note from the Carnation Milk company informing her that she had won first prize in their limerick contest. The note went on to say that unfortunately, the company would not be able to publish her limerick. This puzzled her because she did not remember sending in a limerick. She did remember starting one and putting it aside. The first two lines were:

Carnation Milk, the best in the land
I hold a can right here in my hand.

She asked her teenage son. He had spent the summer working on a farm. He explained that he had, indeed, added the three final lines to the limerick. The last three lines of the winning limerick were:

No teats to pull
No dung to pitch
Just punch a hole in the son of a bitch.

Telephone Survey

The cost of a **telephone survey** is greater than that of a mail survey, but less than that of a face-to-face survey. Telephone surveys tend to have high response rates, the information can be collected in a relatively short time, and respondents feel some anonymity. Another advantage is that for a telephone survey you do not need a list of all of the people in the population.

High response rates can be attributed to a number of factors. First, most people, if they are home, will answer the telephone rather than let it ring. Once they answer the phone they are usually willing to spend some time talking, unless they are in the middle of some other task. (No one knows, however, what the impact of telephone answering machines will be on the response rate for telephone surveys.) A second factor contributing to high telephone survey response rates—even higher than for face-to-face surveys—is that a phone caller is less threatening than a stranger at the door. People are often loath to let strangers into their home, particularly if they are alone. A telephone surveyor, no matter what gender or size, is not a physical threat.

Telephone surveys also are quicker to conduct than are mail or face-to-face surveys. The surveyor places the call and gets an immediate response. With mail surveys you have no control over when people fill out the questionnaire. It may sit on a kitchen table for a week or questionnaires may come back six to eight weeks after they are sent out. With a telephone survey, if the person is not home, the surveyor calls the next number on the list and tries the first number again later. Face-to-face surveyors lose time traveling to individual respondents, particularly if the respondents live in rural areas.

Respondents to a telephone survey feel some anonymity because they are not looking at (nor being watched by) the interviewer. Under these circumstances, respondents may feel more comfortable answering threatening questions. For instance, some early surveys of alcohol consumption found that women who were interviewed through the mail or over the telephone were more likely to admit to drinking alcoholic beverages than were women who were interviewed personally.

One problem with telephone surveys that may have already occurred to you is that not everyone has a telephone. Are we obtaining a biased sample if we limit ourselves to people with telephones? The answer is, probably not. In most states and provinces in North America, at least 95 percent of households have telephones.

Telephone surveys do have some limitations. One is the type of question that can be asked; another is how long the interview can take. When you ask questions over the telephone, you cannot expect people to choose among complex alternatives. Can you imagine taking a multiple-choice examination over the telephone? You would have to remember each alternative while the interviewer read you the others. Then you would have to select the best one from those you remembered. Thus, telephone survey questions must be kept fairly simple.

Many people are surprised at the length of time respondents are willing to spend answering questions on the telephone. A thirty-minute questionnaire is probably near the upper limit of a person's patience, but some telephone surveys have taken forty-five minutes. Most people like being surveyed. It is flattering that someone wants to know your opinion. How many times has someone sat down with you, asked you questions, and listened to your answers without arguing with you? However, the extensive use of telemarketing techniques may reduce people's willingness to respond to telephone surveys.

A combination of mail and telephone surveys can enable a researcher to overcome some of the limitations of telephone surveys.

One strategy is to mail the survey to a respondent and inform them that you will be telephoning them at a particular time to get their answers. This allows the researcher to ask questions that have complex alternatives. It also allows the respondent to think about and research answers to some of the questions. For instance, a respondent might have to check records to answer a question about volume of sales in the previous year.

Face-to-Face Surveys

We have implicitly discussed many of the advantages and disadvantages of **face-to-face surveys** when we considered the advantages and disadvantages of other survey methods. With face-to-face surveys you can ask complicated questions; you can be sure that the respondent is the person sampled; and if the person is not literate, the surveyor can read the questions out loud. In a face-to-face situation, the interviewer can take note of subtle, non-verbal cues from the respondent. For instance, the interviewer can judge if a respondent understands a question.

In many third-world countries, such as those in South America, Asia and Africa, the face-to-face survey may be the only method suitable for conducting a survey. In these places most people do not have telephones and there may be a high rate of illiteracy.

As you can imagine, conducting a face-to-face survey is costly in terms of time and money. The response rate depends a great deal on the person doing the interviewing, as well as the training afforded the interviewers beforehand. Even if you conduct the survey in a North American city, it takes time for the interviewer to travel to the respondents' homes or offices for the interview. If the respondent is not home, the interviewer may have to return later. If the respondent lives in rural or sparsely settled areas, travel may take even longer. If we pay the interviewer by the hour, it can be very expensive.

Summary

When a population is very large, a researcher will usually select a sample of persons to interview. The sample can be selected using a probability or a nonprobability procedure. In a probability sample, all elements of a population have the same likelihood of being included. In a nonprobability sample, there is no way to estimate the likelihood of any single element being selected.

There are two nonprobability sampling procedures, accidental and purposive. In an accidental sample, the first people encountered are included in the sample. Serious researchers rarely use an accidental sample. In a purposive sample, the most interesting or informative people are selected. Purposive sampling is used more frequently by anthropologists and sociologists than by psychologists.

There are three types of probability sampling procedures: simple random, stratified random, and multi-stage. Simple random sampling involves randomly selecting elements from a list of the entire population. Stratified random sampling involves dividing the population into subgroups and then randomly sampling elements from each subgroup. Multi-stage sampling involves a series of simple random samples taken from successively smaller portions of the population. Random-digit dialing is a method of sampling telephone numbers that does not require a sampling frame and one that can be used in conjunction with any of the other probability sampling procedures.

Deciding on an appropriate sample size is not easy. There are theoretical guidelines for the appropriate size and there are practical constraints. For most nonprofessional surveyors, practical constraints such as time and money dictate the size of the sample.

At the same time researchers consider the sample, they also must consider the best way to administer the survey. These two considerations influence each other. Availability of population lists may influence how one administers the questionnaire, and at the same time, how one wants to administer the questionnaire may influence how one samples.

In table 7.3 we have summarized the advantages and disadvantages of each of the methods. As you can see, each method of administering a survey has advantages and disadvantages. As you can also tell, in most circumstances we prefer the telephone survey.

TABLE 7.3 Advantages and Disadvantages of each Method of Administering Surveys

Method	Advantages	Disadvantages
Mail survey	—Inexpensive —Anonymous	—May take weeks to get responses —Low response rate (may lead to biased sample) —Cannot be sure who filled out the questionnaire —Need list of addresses
Telephone survey	—Moderately expensive —Some anonymity —High response rate —Quick —Do not need list of members of population	—Survey cannot be too long —Cannot use questions with multiple alternative responses
Face-to-face survey	—Only way to reach some populations —Interviewer can pay attention to nonverbal behavior —Survey can be longer than telephone survey —Can tell who fills out questionnaire —Response rate is good with well trained interviewer	—Expensive —Need list of members of population

Anything New?

Research Methods: Some Things Don't Change

In this chapter we will consider changes that have taken place in social psychological research design in the last twenty-five years. We will first consider alternatives to deception that have been explored. Then we will look at a study that examined research in social psychology since 1968.

Alternatives to Deception

In chapters 1 and 2 we spoke about deception in experiments as a way of reducing threats to external validity. We indicated that many social psychologists are unhappy using deception in their research. One alternative that has been explored is *simulation research*. In the 1960s and early 1970s social psychologists explored two simulation methods, *role playing* and *game playing*. More recently some social psychologists have been exploring a third simulation method, *computer simulation*. We will briefly describe these procedures and then examine their use today.

Role Playing

Kelman (1967) was concerned about the unquestioning use of deception in social psychology experiments in the late 1960s. Rather than designing elaborate scenarios to fool subjects, Kelman suggested a simple **role playing** alternative. With this method a situation would be described to subjects who would then be asked to play a role and to behave in the way that a person in that situation would behave. (Subjects would not be told the hypothesis.) In other words, the subject is asked to *simulate* being another person and *simulate* behavior in a hypothetical situation.

Rosenberg and Abelson (1960) used a role-playing procedure to investigate cognitive imbalance. Subjects were told that the purpose of the experiment was to see how well they could put themselves in someone else's position. They were to try to respond to a problem situation as they thought the other person would—they were to "try to *be* this man." (See p. 124.)

Subjects were told to imagine that they owned a large department store and wanted to keep sales as high as possible. One third of the subjects were told that they liked Fenwick, the manager of the rug department, and also that they liked modern art. Another third of the subjects were told that they liked Fenwick but disliked modern art. Finally, the remaining subjects were told that they disliked both Fenwick and modern art.

All subjects were further told:

a) that a recent survey had indicated that modern art was disliked by most lower and middle class customers and might lower sales if exhibited in stores;

b) that Fenwick planned to mount a modern art display in his department; and

c) that in his three years in the rug department Fenwick had established a solid reputation as an effective sales manager.

Based on this information subjects were placed in an unbalanced situation (cf., Heider, 1958). They were then presented with communications and evidence designed to reduce this imbalance. One communication contended that modern art actually increased sales, the second contended that Fenwick did not really intend to display modern art, and the third argued that Fenwick was not really an effective manager.

Imagine a subject who is told she likes Fenwick, Fenwick is an effective manager, but he intends to display modern art. Displaying modern art, which will reduce sales, is not balanced with the first two concepts. There are several ways the three communications can help her reduce this imbalance. She could decide that Fenwick really hasn't been an effective manager. If she does this, however, she is still left with the fact that sales are going to be reduced, and to restore balance, she would also have to decide that high sales are not important. In short, the subject would have to change two cognitions. But if she decides that modern art does not reduce sales, balance is achieved and no further cognitive changes are needed. Thus, Rosenberg and Abelson argued, the communication that modern art does not reduce sales restores balance with the least effort.

After reading the communications, subjects rated each on how much it pleased them, how much it persuaded them, and finally, how accurate it appeared to them. Rosenberg and Abelson hypothesized that for each combination of concepts and information, the communication which involved least effort in reducing imbalance would be rated most highly. They found that in general, this was correct. The communication which let subjects restore imbalance with the least effort was rated most pleasing, accurate, and persuasive.

Some researchers were strongly in favor of role playing as an alternative to deception (Ring, 1967; Schultz, 1969) while others (Aronson et al., 1990; McGuire, 1967; Freedman, 1969) were equally strongly against it. Two problems with role playing were cited most often. First, many role players may simply respond in what they think is the socially acceptable manner. Second, role players may not be capable of predicting how they would behave, particularly in situations they have never experienced.

Social psychologists who opposed role playing argued that a role-playing subject simply engages in guesswork. Freedman (1969) suggested that when an experimenter's hypothesis is confirmed in this kind of study, all that has been shown is that the experimenter's guesses are similar to those of the subjects.

The inability to predict one's own behavior in a real situation is illustrated in a study by Ebbesen and Konecni (1975). They investigated the information which influences a judge's decision when setting bail. In the first part of their experiment, real judges were presented with simulated cases. In these cases, background variables of an accused person were systematically varied. The judges were asked what bail they would set for the accused. Analysis of their answers indicated that for the simulated cases, the judges' decisions were determined by (a) the accused's previous criminal record and

(b) the extent to which the accused had ties to the community (for instance, how long the accused had lived in the community or whether the accused had family in the area).

When many of the same judges were subsequently observed in real trial settings, the amount of bail was found to be determined almost exclusively by the district attorney's recommendation (which in turn, was determined almost completely by the severity of the crime). Thus, when making decisions in real situations, the judges' decisions were not based on the same criteria they used in the simulated conditions.

Ebbesen and Konecni compared each judge's role-playing behavior with his actual behavior. A few researchers have found that the results obtained from role-playing subjects are similar to those obtained from deceived subjects (Greenberg, 1967; Darroch & Steiner, 1970; Horowitz & Rothschild, 1970; Willis & Willis, 1970). However, Miller (1972) has pointed to flaws in the design and interpretation of the results of each of these experiments. One of Miller's most telling points is that even if role-playing and deception procedures do yield the same results, these results may not reflect the same causal processes. For instance, a person may conform in a role-playing experiment in order to cooperate with the experimenter, while a person may conform in a deception experiment because of perceived peer pressure. In this example the results of an experimental manipulation of group size would likely lead to different results.

An experiment by Holmes and Bennet (1974) compared the physiological reactions of deceived subjects with those of role-playing subjects. In the first of their three experimental conditions, subjects were told that they were going to receive electric shocks (stress group). In the second condition, subjects were asked to play the role of subjects who were going to receive electric shocks (role-playing group). It was explained to them that they would not actually receive any shocks. In the third condition, electric shocks were not mentioned to the subjects (no-stress group).

The subjects' verbal reports of anxiety were not significantly different in the stress and the role-playing groups, and both groups reported higher anxiety than did the no-stress group. On the other hand, physiological measures of arousal (pulse and respiration) indicated that only the stress group was aroused. There was no difference between the role-playing and the no-stress groups in physiological arousal. There is another interesting side note to this study, relevant to the effect of debriefing on previously deceived subjects. After debriefing, physiological arousal of subjects in the stress condition appeared to drop from its initially high level to the same level as that of subjects in the no-stress condition.

Miller (1972) pointed out, as did Freedman (1969), that the question of deception versus role playing is not one which will be answered on the basis of experiments comparing the two procedures. The question is an epistemological one. What body of data is most appropriate for social psychology?

Role playing quietly disappeared from the published social psychological literature after the flurry of activity in the late 1960s and early 1970s. It is not clear why this happened. No one experiment led to its demise.

Game Playing

When people play games they often become very involved in them. Even though the stakes may be imaginary, people behave as if they are real. (Or it may be that there are psychological stakes, like increased status, that *are* real.) Some social psychologists use game playing as a model for behavior when the stakes are real. This kind of **game-playing simulation** procedure has been used most extensively in studies of bargaining and decision making. The types of games used have ranged from pencil and paper matrices to elaborate electronic games.

Deutsch and Krauss (1962) reported one of the earliest game-playing simulations. They investigated the effect of threat on interpersonal bargaining using a trucking game. The two opponents had to reach a destination along a path which could accommodate only one of them at a time. The opponents were each assigned a fictitious trucking company, Acme or Bolt, and were told that each company's goal was to make as large a profit as possible.

In order to make a profit, the opponents, representing their respective companies, had to travel from their origin to their destination in less than sixty seconds. Beyond that, money was subtracted from their earnings. If they took an outer, winding road, the destination could not be reached in under sixty seconds. The middle road, while allowing the trip to be completed in under sixty seconds, could not accommodate both trucks at once.

Although subjects were told to make as large a profit as possible, the dependent measure was their combined profits. Strategically, the shorter the time it took the two companies to achieve a cooperative solution to the problem, the higher would be their combined profit. Deutsch and Krauss found that when neither Acme nor

Bolt had the ability to threaten the other, their combined profits were greatest—i.e., they rapidly arrived at a mutually beneficial agreement. When one of the two companies had the option of threatening the other (by blocking the middle road with a gate) profits were intermediate. When both companies had the threat option, profit was lowest. Subjects in this situation rarely arrived at a mutually beneficial agreement.

Another game simulation which has been used extensively to investigate decision making in conflict situations is the **prisoner's dilemma.** In this dilemma, a person is presented with the following situation:

> You and your partner in crime are arrested and immediately put in separate cells so that you cannot communicate with each other. The prosecuting attorney visits each of you and tells you that if neither of you confesses there is enough evidence to convict you and send you to jail for 3 years. If one of you is willing to confess, you will be let off with only 2 years but your partner, who remained silent, will go to jail for 7 years. If, however, you both confess in order to get a lighter sentence, you will both go to jail for 5 years.

Researchers have created laboratory analogues of this situation and have varied the possible outcomes to determine the parameters which affect peoples' decisions to cooperate (by keeping quiet) or to compete (by confessing). The prisoners' dilemma is a **mixed-motive game** in that there are pressures on people both to compete and to cooperate.

Another mixed-motive situation in which subjects engage in a kind of simulation is the **commons dilemma.** This dilemma occurs when a group of people try to manage a scarce but renewable resource (or when the people must decide whether or not to contribute to some common resource, Brewer & Kramer, 1986). Let us assume that (a) there are one hundred units of some resource in the environment, (b) that what is left in the environment at the end of one season will double before the beginning of the next season, and (c) that the resource has an upper limit of two hundred units.

Each person in the group is allowed to take as much or as little of the resource in each season as he wishes, and each person's yearly income is heavily dependent upon the number of resource units which can be harvested. The more each person takes, the less there will be for the other people and the less there will be in next year's supply. The problem is not just whether to delay gratification: the outcomes also depend on other people's decisions. For instance, a person might decide to take a small amount to let the resource grow. However, one of the other group members might take everything that was left, leaving nothing to grow for the next year. If you think about this situation you will realize that the best strategy for the group as a whole is to allow the resource to build to its maximum size (this can be done most quickly by not harvesting any units in the first season) and then to take a total of one hundred units in each subsequent season. In this way the resource can be made to last indefinitely and to yield its maximum return year after year. Ideally, the one hundred units harvested each season would be divided equally among the group members so that each member's wealth would grow steadily at the same rate.

How do groups behave when faced with this kind of situation? It usually does not take people very long to figure out what the best strategy for the group *should* be, but some groups have a great deal of trouble ensuring that all their members adhere to this strategy for the common good. One member, for example, may take more than his or her share. Other members then may retaliate either by doing the same (Schroeder et al., 1983), or by imposing some penalty on the defector (Sato, 1987). If some kinds of retaliatory behavior go unchecked, the result may be that the group will draw too much out of the environment, the replenishment before the next season will be reduced, and in some cases the resource may be totally depleted.

Jorgenson and Papciak (1981) have found that laboratory groups generally do best at maintaining a resource when there is clear information about the state of the resource and when members are able to communicate freely with one another. In addition, it appears to help if subjects (a) have some experience as individuals in managing the resource (Allison & Messick, 1985), and (b) are encouraged to think in terms of the larger collective rather than in terms of characteristics on which members or subgroups can be differentiated (Kramer & Brewer, 1984).

Unfortunately, the conditions that are most conducive to rational resource management do not always exist in the real world. Take a natural resource like the North Atlantic cod fishery, for example. There is considerable uncertainty about the state of the resource, the replenishment factor is unknown and probably fluctuates because of natural factors, communication among the various groups involved is poor, and often there is little possibility of careful monitoring and control of harvesting behavior.

One difficulty with the game simulation technique as an alternative to deception is its limited applicability. While it is a useful vehicle for the investigation of bargaining and cooperative/competitive decision making, it does not lend itself to research in areas such as attitude change or helping.

A second and more important problem with the use of game simulations is the assumption that people's behavior in game situations is similar to their behavior in nongame situations. Deutsch and Krauss (1962) found that bilateral threat made it nearly impossible for subjects to reach a cooperative solution to their problem. However, Gallo (1966) found that when a similar game situation used real rather than "make believe" money, subjects had little difficulty achieving a mutually beneficial agreement no matter what the threat conditions. In real life other motives may become preeminent. To complicate the picture, behavior does not change when you use real money in a prisoner's dilemma situation.

As we said earlier, we consider both role playing and game playing to be simulations. The major difference between the two seems to be in the amount of experimental realism a subject experiences. Game playing has a great deal of experimental realism, role playing—at least the way it has been used by social psychologists—does not. This might be because we all have considerable practice at playing games, but little at role playing.

Social psychologists have viewed simulation as a research tool. That is, they have seen it as a way to study behavior while people were engaged in a task, such as playing a game. Apart from its application in studying bargaining, cooperation, and competition, game playing has not been used extensively. In the 1968 edition (Abelson) of the *Handbook of Social Psychology* there was a chapter on simulation; in the most recent edition (Lindzey & Aronson, 1985) this chapter has been dropped.

Computer Simulation

In the case of **computer simulation,** the simulation technique is a theoretical aid not an empirical tool. In this sense computer models are used as alternatives not just to deception procedures but to empirical testing of hypotheses in general.

Although computer simulation has not been used much by social psychologists, it has been used extensively by cognitive psychologists to study intellectual processes, such as solving problems and making decisions. In cognitive psychology it has been used as a way of developing and exploring models of how humans think. Recently some social psychologists (e.g., Nowak, Szamrej, & Latané, 1990; Ostrom, 1988; Stasser, 1988) have advocated computer simulation as a way of developing models and testing theories about social behavior.

Ostrom (1988) distinguished among three symbol systems that can be used to communicate theories—verbal, mathematical, and computer simulation. Using computer simulation to communicate forces a theorist to be more precise. By translating from a verbal description to a computer program, a person becomes aware of areas of the theory that are not clear and areas where there may be inconsistencies. It is not the computer simulation *per se* that leads to greater precision. It is, as Hastie (1988) noted, the need to write the simulation in programming language that leads to the theory being "*. . . clear . . . concrete . . . complete . . .* and internally *consistent. . . .*" (See p. 425—italics in original.) A computer simulation can also generate testable predictions.

Nowak and colleagues (1990) believed that as a research tool, computer simulations can provide social psychologists with a bridge between individual behavior and group behavior. For instance, a computer simulation can help us understand how the information that an individual recalls can influence and be influenced by group discussion. Ostrom (1988) also envisioned a role for computer simulations in helping us to understand complex behavior and dynamic interactions among variables that verbal theories have not been able to encompass. For instance, most theories deal with one variable in one situation at a time. However, social behavior occurs in many different situations in many guises. As Ostrom noted, attitudes can take many forms and influence behavior in different ways in different situations.

Two potential problems are posed by computer simulations. First, outcomes depend on inputs. As computer programmers note, "Garbage in, garbage out." As long as the results of the computer simulation are evaluated by comparison with empirical findings, this is not a problem.

The second potential problem is the growth of unnecessarily complex theories using computer simulation. As Ostrom (1988) noted, it is easy to add variables and computer routines and to make theories more complex than necessary. Similarly, if predictions do not match results, it may be tempting to add a new variable or routine to fit the results. This problem, of course, is not unique to computer simulation models.

Changes in Research Methods, 1968 to 1988.

West, Newsom, and Fenaughty (1992) analyzed a random selection of articles that had appeared in the *Journal of Personality and Social Psychology* (*JPSP*) in 1968 and 1988.[1] For the two samples, they compared the research designs, types of subjects used, how the independent variables were manipulated, and how the dependent variables were measured.

West and colleagues (1992) divided research designs into six types: (1) meta and secondary analysis, (2) cross-sectional, (3) longitudinal, (4) experimental-personality, (5) quasi-experiments, and (6) true experiments. It is interesting to note that neither role playing nor simulations appear as possible designs at either time. We have talked about most of these designs, but in some cases we have used slightly different names. Cross-sectional designs refer to observational studies—studies where the experimenter does not manipulate any of the variables. These would include studies using unobtrusive measures and studies we have categorized as case studies. Longitudinal designs include studies where observations are made more than once—for instance, studies using cross-lagged correlations.

The study by West and colleagues (1992) also distinguished between true experimental designs and experimental-personality designs. A study in which the experimenter manipulates all independent variables and all subjects are randomly assigned to conditions is classed as a true experiment. A study in which the experimenter measures one independent variable and manipulates one independent variable (with random assignment to conditions) is classed as an experimental-personality design. An example of an experimental-personality design might be a study that included gender or age as one of the independent variables.

As can be seen in table 8.1A, in twenty years little has changed in the design of studies reported in *JPSP*. Most researchers still do true experiments. Much less common are cross-sectional and experimental-personality designs. Similarly, there has been little change in the population from which subjects are selected. West and colleagues (1992) found that the great majority of the studies reported in both 1968 and 1988 used undergraduate students (see table 8.1B).

---

1. JPSP was selected because Reis and Stiller (1992) used the journal for a similar historical comparison. Reis and Stiller (p. 466) in turn selected JPSP because, "it consistently receives the highest impact scores (i.e., average citation per published article) and quality ratings of personality and social psychology journals."

TABLE 8.1A–C.	Changes in Research Reported in *Journal of Personality and Social Psychology* from 1968 to 1988		

A. Design type		1968	1988
	Meta and secondary analysis	4%	9%
	Cross-sectional	20%	24%
	Longitudinal	0%	5%
	Experimental-personality	22%	18%
	Quasi-experiment	7%	0%
	True experiment	47%	44%
B. Subject population			
	Undergraduates	72%	80%
	School children	17%	0%
	Adults in community	6%	12%
	Special populations	6%	8%
C. Manipulation of independent variable			
	1. Written or oral instructions	60%	41%
	2. Written description, photo	13%	24%
	3. False feedback	26%	18%
	4. Audio or videotaped segment	8%	9%
	5. Interaction with confederate	20%	5%
	6. Interaction with actual subject	8%	9%

From West, S. G., Newsom, J. T., & Fenaughty, A. M. (1992). Publication trends in JPSP: Stability and change in topics, methods and theories across two decades, in *Personality and Social Psychology Bulletin, 18* (pp. 473–484). Copyright © 1992 Sage Publications. Reprinted by permission of Sage Publications, Inc.

Independent variables were categorized into six groups, reflecting the power of the manipulation. By "power" the researchers were referring to the manipulation's realism or impact. The categories and the percentage of studies using the manipulations can be seen in table 8.1C.

Overall, at both times, most studies used written or oral instructions, the least powerful manipulation. The only category in which there was a significant change was in "Interaction with confederate." The percentage of studies using this second-most-powerful manipulation decreased from 20 percent to 5 percent. It also is

TABLE 8.2 Types of Dependent Measures Used in
1968 and 1988

	1968	1988
Clinical interview	2%	4%
Self report	55%	82%
Behavior coding	9%	20%
Physiological	0%	4%
Behavior count	60%	28%

From West, S. G., Newsom, J. T., & Fenaughty, A. M. (1992), Publication trends in JPSP: Stability and change in topics, methods and theories across two decades, in *Personality and Social Psychology Bulletin, 18*, (pp. 473–484). Copyright © 1992 Sage Publications. Reprinted with the permission of Sage Publications, Inc.

interesting to note that there was no significant change in the percent of studies in which the investigator checked on the independent manipulation (26 percent in 1968 and 32 percent in 1988).

Dependent measures were categorized into (1) clinical interview/Thematic Apperception Test measures, (2) self reports and questionnaire measures, (3) behavior coding, (4) physiological measures, and (5) behavior counts. Both behavior coding and, to a lesser degree, behavior counts require trained observers. In behavior coding an observer must interpret a subject's response—for instance, decide if a response was aggressive. In the case of behavior counts, less interpretation is required of an observer. For instance, an observer might count the number of passersby who walk between two people who are speaking.

The outcome of the analysis is shown in table 8.2. As can be seen, there was a significant increase in the percentage of the studies using self reports and a significant decrease in the percentage using behavior counts. There was also a slight increase in the percentage of studies using behavior coding.

Based on results of West and colleagues we would conclude that little changed in research methods between 1968 and 1988. Further, when the changes did occur, they were in the direction of weaker manipulations and greater reliance on self report measures.

Summary

In general, social psychologists have been unhappy using deception in their research. This has led them to explore alternative procedures. Three simulation alternatives have been explored: role playing, game playing, and computer simulation. In a role-playing procedure, a situation is described to subjects and they are asked to behave as though they were in that situation. Role playing quietly disappeared from the published social psychological literature after a flurry of activity in the late 1960s and early 1970s. It is not clear why this happened, but serious criticisms of the method may have played some part.

Game-playing studies have been used to increase our understanding of bargaining and decision-making behavior in conflict situations where the stakes are real. Despite its application in these areas, the game-playing procedure is receiving relatively little current use. In the 1968 (Abelson) edition of the *Handbook of Social Psychology* there was a chapter on simulation; in the most recent edition (Lindzey & Aronson, 1985) this chapter was dropped.

We consider both role playing and game playing to be simulations. The major difference between the two seems to be in their degree of experimental realism. Game-playing procedures have a great deal of experimental realism, while role-playing procedures—at least the way they have been used by social psychologists—do not.

Social psychologists have viewed simulation as a research tool. That is, they have seen it as a way to study behavior while people were engaged in a task, such as playing a game. In the case of computer simulation, the simulation technique is a theoretical aid more than an empirical tool. Recently some social psychologists have advocated computer simulation as a way of developing models and testing theories about social behavior.

A review of research methods between 1968 and 1988 indicated little change in the design of studies reported in the *Journal of Personality and Social Psychology*. Most researchers still draw their subjects from college-student populations, still use the experimental method, still use written or oral instructions to manipulate the independent variable, and still rely on self-report measures to assess the effect on the dependent variable.

Meta-Analysis: New Methods of Analyzing Old Data

In the earlier chapters of this book we considered what may be called *primary research methods*. With these methods, the researcher formulates an hypothesis, designs a study to test it, gathers the data, and interprets the results. Researchers do not, however, work in isolation. The hypotheses they develop and the interpretations they give to the outcomes of their own work depend heavily on the published work of others. In fact, a large part of any researcher's time is spent studying and drawing conclusions from the research literature.

Drawing conclusions from the literature is not an easy task. Published studies come from many different sources. Given the number of choices that a researcher must make about design, procedures, and methods of analysis, the diversity one finds in published studies is hardly surprising. It can be disconcerting, however, when one finds diversity not just in the methods but in the outcomes as well. Tests of the same hypothesis sometimes yield results that support the hypothesis, sometimes results that refute it, and sometimes, results which fail to reach statistical significance in either direction. How can one make sense of such inconsistency?

Faced with inconsistent results in the research literature, researchers in earlier times were forced to rely on subjective judgments, perhaps supplemented by crude methods of description and summary (e.g., "The majority of studies in this area have found that . . ."). More recently researchers have begun to use sophisticated statistical methods that allow them to combine the results of several independent studies and arrive at conclusions with a precisely stated degree of confidence. The term **meta-analysis** is used to refer to these methods. In the present chapter, we will try to give you some idea of what these methods involve. Our emphasis will be on what meta-analysis is rather than on how to do it. If you are interested in conducting a meta-analysis, you should consult one or more of the several excellent texts on the subject that are now available (e.g., Hedges & Olkin, 1985; Hunter & Schmidt, 1990; Rosenthal, 1984).

It is possible to view meta-analysis not just as a set of statistical techniques, but more broadly, as a quantitative approach to reviewing and integrating research findings (see Bangert-Drowns, 1986). In fact, meta-analysis can be viewed as a kind of research endeavor in itself and an alternative to other, primary research strategies. From this perspective, many analogies can be drawn between meta-analysis and the research methods that we have already considered. Like the other methods, meta-analysis is better suited to some kinds of research questions than others, and like the other methods, it is susceptible to certain kinds of biases and difficulties in interpretation. We will stress the parallels between meta-analysis and other research methods as we consider each of the stages in the meta-analytic approach.

In our discussion of replications in chapter 3, we briefly mentioned a meta-analytic review of the literature on the attitude-memory relationship, conducted by Roberts (1985). Throughout our description of meta-analysis, we will use Roberts' study as an example.

TABLE 9.1 Recent Examples of Meta-analyses Published in the *Psychological Bulletin*

1. Gender differences in mathematics performance (Hyde, Fennema, & Lamon, 1990)
2. Gender and leadership style (Eagly & Johnson, 1990)
3. Antecedents, correlates, and consequences of organizational commitment (Mathieu & Zajac, 1990)
4. Subjective well-being interventions among elders (Okun, Olding, & Cohn, 1990)
5. Sex differences in the course of personality development (Cohn, 1991)
6. Parents' differential socialization of boys and girls (Lytton & Romney, 1991)
7. Effectiveness of cognitive-behavior therapy for maladapting children (Durlak, Fuhrman, & Lampman, 1991)
8. Validity of questionnaire and TAT measures of Need for Achievement (Spangler, 1992)
9. Gender and the evaluation of leaders (Eagly, Makhijani, & Klonsky, 1992)
10. Parental divorce and the well-being of children (Amato & Keith, 1991)

Defining the Research Question or Hypothesis

Meta-analysis can be used for a wide range of research questions or hypotheses. The examples of meta-analytic reviews shown in table 9.1, all published since January, 1990 in the *Psychological Bulletin*, indicate the range of problems to which this method has been applied.

Roberts (1985) carried out a meta-analysis to determine whether or not people learned material more quickly and retained it longer, if the material supported their attitudes. He began by specifying four different ways in which the selective-learning hypothesis could be investigated. First, using some measure of memory or learning, one could look for evidence of a statistical interaction between direction of people's attitudes (pro or con) and direction of the material to be learned. Second, one could draw a simple comparison between the rates with which attitude-supportive and nonsupportive information is learned and retained. Third, agreement ratings of attitude statements could be correlated with recall of those statements at a later time. Finally, one might separate subjects who show selective learning from those who do not and then search for other variables which distinguish the two groups. Roberts searched the literature for instances of all four of these approaches.

As Roberts study and the examples in table 9.1 suggest, the research questions in meta-analytic reviews are generally straight-forward. The meta-analyst's questions or hypotheses need not be the same as the ones that prompted the original studies. For example, in meta-analyses of gender differences, any study can be included as long as the original authors provided either a breakdown of their data by gender or sufficient information for such a breakdown. For the original authors, gender differences may have been of little or no interest.

There are research questions for which meta-analysis may not be useful. If the research question is a highly novel one or if the hypothesis concerns a complex interaction among variables rarely studied together, then a meta-analytic review of the literature is un-likely to be of much help. In more heavily worked areas, however, meta-analysis should be routinely considered when literature reviews are undertaken.

Deciding which Studies to Include

There is a sense in which a meta-analysis is like a survey. The survey researcher must decide on the appropriate population and on the methods to be used to obtain a representative sample from that population. Similarly, the meta-analyst must decide on the population of studies to be reviewed and on criteria for including or excluding particular studies. Obviously, selected studies must provide information about the hypothesis of interest, but beyond this, several other factors need to be considered. Should the population to review be limited to studies published in journals or should doctoral dissertations, conference presentations, and unpublished manuscripts be included? What about studies where potentially useful information was apparently collected but not reported? Should the author(s) be contacted and asked to provide the information? This question is analogous to the one that faces the survey researcher who must decide how relentlessly to pursue respondents who are difficult to contact. In both types of research, the decisions that are made can affect the potential for systematic biases in the results.

In survey research, each member of the population should have an equal chance of being included in the sample but the same is not always true in meta-analytic research where judgments about the *quality* of studies may be part of the selection criteria. One can argue, for example, that published studies, having undergone peer review, are likely to be of better quality than unpublished ones. Conversely, if only published studies are included, there may be a bias toward studies where statistically significant results were obtained. In this connection, Rosenthal (1979) has talked about the **file-drawer problem.** For every study with significant results that appears in the journals, there may be countless other "failures" in researchers' file drawers.

Even published studies can vary widely in quality. Should studies of questionable internal validity (i.e., with apparent methodological flaws) be included in a meta-analytic review of the literature? Should external validity be a selection criterion? Meta-analysts are not entirely in agreement on questions such as these. Those who favor more restrictive inclusion requirements point to the obvious difficulties in interpreting the results of flawed studies. Those who favor less strict inclusion requirements point to the subjective nature of methodological judgments and the potential for systematic bias by the researcher (analogous to experimenter bias in laboratory research). Between these two positions is one taken by more empirically minded meta-analysts who argue that (a) lenient inclusion standards permit systematic comparisons later between studies that do and do not share a particular methodological weakness, and (b) if studies are to be screened for quality, such judgments should be made by persons who are unaware of the meta-analyst's hypotheses and the judgments should be subjected to the usual tests for inter-rater reliability and validity (cf., chapter 4).

In his search of the literature on the attitude-memory relationship, Roberts (1985) restricted his search to the published literature (including dissertations), using key words that appeared in the subject index of the *Psychological Abstracts.* The reference lists of the studies that turned up were searched for further appropriate references. In addition, all social psychology textbooks from 1908 to 1983 in the University of Toronto library were searched for references. Roberts justified his exclusion of unpublished manuscripts by arguing that (a) the number of such manuscripts in this particular area was likely to be small, and (b) the inclusion of unpublished studies would lower the quality of the data base and introduce an element of subjectivity into the selection procedure. In total, Roberts found thirty-eight studies that met his requirements.

Examining the Critical Variables

Independent and Dependent Variables

Like most researchers, the meta-analyst will usually define the independent and dependent variables in conceptual rather than operational terms. For example, an investigator may wish to compare the effects of authoritarian and democratic leadership styles on group morale. In other kinds of research, the researcher would go on to choose what seemed to be the most appropriate ways to operationalize the variables. In meta-analysis, the investigator must often deal with a disconcertingly wide variety of operationalizations chosen by other researchers (see chapter 3 for our earlier discussion of conceptual replications). In some cases, an authoritarian leader may be defined as one who acts in an aloof, critical manner. In other cases, such a leader may be defined simply as one who makes decisions without consultation. Similarly, group morale may sometimes be defined in terms of members' satisfaction with the leader, sometimes in terms of their liking for each other, and sometimes in terms of their willingness to continue meeting together. If several different operationalizations have been used in the same study, the meta- analyst must decide whether to (a) select just the operationalization that seems most appropriate, (b) examine the results for each operationalization separately, perhaps coding the results for later comparisons, or (c) combine the results of the different operationalizations into a single test.

Moderator Variables

Often, the meta-analyst will have an hypothesis not just about the existence of a relationship between two variables, but also about other variables that may moderate the strength of that relationship. For example, an authoritarian leader may evoke high group morale when the group task is simple and easily completed, but may evoke conflict when the group task is more difficult. Almost always, meta-analysts will include information about a number of variables that, for theoretical reasons, may be expected to moderate the relationship of primary interest.

It may also be important for the analyses to include aspects of the design and procedure of each study that may have influenced the outcome of the hypothesis test. Most important, of course, is the sample size on which the hypothesis test was based. This number is frequently used as a weighting factor when the results of different studies are combined. In addition, one may wish to record whether a between- or within-subject design was used, as well as some index of impact or realism of the experimental manip- ulation that was used. Finally, in some cases, meta-analysts will assign a quality score to each study that, like the sample size, can be used as a weighting factor. In these cases, the outcomes of the "better" studies can be weighted more heavily. This, however, is a controversial procedure. The basis for qualitative judgments has to be clearly stated and vigorously defended.

In addition to examining the critical attitude-memory relationship reported in each study, Roberts (1985) noted several other characteristics of each study that, for theoretical reasons, he thought might affect the strength of the attitude-memory relationship. For example, the length of the material being learned, the attitudinal issue, the length of the retention interval, and whether the learning was deliberate or incidental were noted for each study. The type of research design and the number of subjects used were also recorded.

Analyzing the Data

Tests of Statistical Significance

Usually the meta-analyst will be concerned first with a test of the null hypothesis. How likely would the observed results be if there were really no effect? In order to conduct such a test, the results of the different studies must be converted to some common unit. Across the different studies, a variety of test statistics (e.g., t, F, r, χ^2) may have been used. Fortunately, simple formulae exist for converting from one to another (see, for example, Judd, Smith, & Kidder, 1991). Frequently, meta-analysts try to summarize the outcome of each hypothesis test in terms of a standard normal deviate or Z score. These scores can then be averaged and an overall test of significance carried out. This is just one of several techniques that can be used (see, Hedges & Olkin, 1985; Hunter & Schmidt, 1990; Rosenthal, 1984).

Calculating the Fail-Safe Number

We referred earlier to the file-drawer problem. The concern is that for every published study that obtained a statistically significant outcome, there may be several other studies with nonsignificant outcomes that were either turned down by journal editors or not submitted for publication. How many such nonsignificant outcomes would be needed before a meta-analyst's conclusion about a significant effect would be invalidated? This number can be calculated (see Rosenthal, 1979) and is referred to as the **fail-safe** number. Obviously, the larger this number is, the more confident the meta-analyst can be that the observed effect is a real one.

For each of the thirty-eight studies that Roberts (1985) included in his meta-analysis of the attitude-memory relationship, he calculated a t value (more than one if the hypothesis was tested in different ways) that reflected a comparison between memory for attitude-congruent and attitude-incongruent information. These t values were then averaged to obtain an overall Z value (11.07) that was then tested for significance. Roberts (p. 229) concluded that, "There is substantial support for the proposition that people selectively recall attitudinally supportive material." To deal with the file-drawer problem, Roberts calculated the fail-safe number and found it to be 362. There would have to be this number of unpublished studies with null results to nullify the findings obtained in the meta-analysis.

Estimating the Size of the Effect

Meta-analysts, like other researchers, usually try to obtain an indication of the size of the effect, not just its statistical significance. One common method involves expressing the difference between two means in terms of standard deviation units. For instance, the morale in groups with democratic leaders might be found to be 1.2 standard deviations greater than the morale in groups with authoritarian leaders. The size of an effect can also be expressed in terms of the percentage of variance in the dependent variable that is accounted for by the independent variable.

Although Roberts (1985) found that the selective-learning hypothesis had been strongly supported in terms of statistical significance, he went on to examine the size of the effect, using both the d statistic (the difference between means expressed in standard-deviation units) and the point-biserial correlation coefficient. These statistics revealed that the size of the selective-learning effect was relatively small (about one third of a standard deviation) and accounted for only about three percent of the variance in memory recall or recognition scores.

Examining the Role of Moderator Variables

If the size of the effect being examined appears to vary widely across studies (see Hedges & Olkin, 1985, for statistical tests for homogeneity of effect sizes), the role of moderator variables can be examined. For example, regression analyses can be conducted in which the moderator variables are the predictors and effect size is the criterion. The results of analyses such as these can provide the meta-analyst with new hypotheses that can then be tested using primary research methods.

One moderator variable examined by Roberts (1985) was the year in which each study was done. He found that the attitude-memory relationship was more evident in older studies than in recent ones. Apart from this tendency, however, only one other moderator variable—retention interval—seemed to be important. Studies with longer retention intervals tended to show stronger selective-learning effects. This finding suggested to Roberts that reconstructive or rehearsal processes rather than processes that could occur during encoding (e.g., biased attention) are likely responsible for the selective-learning effect. Thus, the meta-analysis not only enabled Roberts to draw some conclusions about the existence and strength of the selective-learning effect, but also about the processes that future investigators should focus on in trying to explain the effect.

Interpreting the Results

Interpreting Statistical Significance and Effect Size

A test of statistical significance tells us whether or not an effect exists but, in itself, it provides little or no information about the strength or importance of the effect. The reason is that the outcome of a significance test depends not just on the size of the effect but also on the number of subjects who were included in the analysis and, more generally, on the overall power of the study. Very powerful studies with large numbers of subjects can detect effects that, although real, may be trivially small. To counteract this problem, researchers who conduct very powerful studies sometimes adopt particularly stringent alpha levels (e.g., .01 or .001) in order to avoid rejecting the null hypothesis with effects of very small size.

An alternative strategy is to examine the effect size directly. How much of the variance in the dependent variable has been accounted for? How great is the separation, in standard deviation units, between the experimental conditions? Guidelines have sometimes been offered to help the researcher decide whether a given effect size is small, medium, or large (see Cohen, 1988). Unfortunately, there is no statistical calculation that will indicate whether an effect is an important one. In experiments in social psychology, for example, the largest effect sizes are typically associated with the findings of least theoretical interest (e.g., checks on the manipulation). We are not suggesting that effect-size statistics should not be calculated, only that they should not be used as substitutes for the informed judgment of the investigator.

Interpreting the Fail-Safe Number

We indicated earlier that the fail-safe number is the number of studies with nonsignificant results that would have to be added to the literature to invalidate a meta-analyst's conclusions about a particular effect. How large should this number be before we place confidence in the obtained result? Rosenthal (1979) suggests that a criterion number can be calculated by multiplying the number of studies included in the review by 5 and then adding 10. If the fail-safe number exceeds this criterion, then the meta-analyst can be reasonably confident that the obtained effect is not likely to be a reflection simply of a publication bias in favor of studies that obtain statistical significance. It should be noted, however, that if there is a publication bias not just against nonsignificant results but also against significant *negative* results (e.g., Mahoney, 1977), then the fail-safe number that is calculated may be misleadingly high. A relatively small number of file-drawer studies with significant negative results could easily invalidate a conclusion about the existence of a positive effect.

Interpreting the Effects of Moderator Variables

Sometimes the most interesting results of a meta-analysis involve relationships between effect size and one or more moderator variables. However, such findings need to be interpreted with the same caution that one normally applies to other findings of a correlational nature. Consider the earlier example concerning the effects of different leadership styles. The difference in morale between groups with democratic and authoritarian leaders may be more evident when the group task is simple, not because of the nature of the task *per se,* but because studies where simple tasks were used also happened to be ones with relatively powerful within-subject designs. In general, when meta-analyses reveal significant relationships involving moderator variables, these should become the focus of subsequent experimental studies that can shed light on the possible causal nature of the relationships.

Summary

In this chapter we have tried to give you some idea of what is involved in conducting a meta-analysis and some of the decisions that a researcher faces when using this technique to summarize and draw conclusions from a body of research. The technique is being used with increasing frequency—a trend most researchers believe is likely to continue. Investigators who are engaged in analyzing and presenting the results of primary research need to keep this in mind. Results should be presented in such a way as to facilitate the task of a meta-analyst who may later want to include the study in a literature review. For example, exact probability values and effect sizes should be routinely reported. In addition, wherever possible, data should be presented in such a way that statistical tests not conducted by the primary researcher can be carried out later by the meta-analyst. Finally, journal editors and reviewers may wish to keep the file-drawer problem in mind when considering studies with unexpected results or results that failed to reach conventional levels of statistical significance.

Codes of Ethics— APA and CPA

American Psychological Association (APA)*

6.06 Planning Research

a. Psychologists design, conduct, and report research in accordance with recognized standards of scientific competence and ethical research.

b. Psychologists plan their research so as to minimize the possibility that results will be misleading.

c. In planning research, psychologists consider its ethical acceptability under the Ethics Code. If an ethical issue is unclear, psychologists seek to resolve the issue through consultation with institutional review boards, animal care and use committees, peer consultations, or other proper mechanisms.

d. Psychologists take reasonable steps to implement appropriate protections for the rights and welfare of human participants, other persons affected by the research, and the welfare of animal subjects.

---

*Copyright 1992 by the American Psychological Association. Adapted by permission.

6.07 Responsibility

    a. Psychologists conduct research competently and with due concern for the dignity and welfare of the participants.

    b. Psychologists are responsible for the ethical conduct of research conducted by them or by others under their supervision or control.

    c. Researchers and assistants are permitted to perform only those tasks for which they are appropriately trained and prepared.

    d. As part of the process of development and implementation of research projects, psychologists consult those with expertise concerning any special population under investigation or most likely to be affected.

6.08 Compliance With Law and Standards

Psychologists plan and conduct research in a manner consistent with federal and state law and regulations, as well as professional standards governing the conduct of research, and particularly those standards governing research with human participants and animal subjects.

6.09 Institutional Approval

Psychologists obtain from host institution or organizations appropriate approval prior to conducting research, and they provide accurate information about their research proposals. They conduct the research in accordance with the approved research protocol.

6.10 Research Responsibilities

Prior to conducting research (except research involving only anonymous surveys, naturalistic observations, or similar research), psychologists enter into an agreement with participants that clarifies the nature of the research and the responsibilities of each party.

6.11 Informed Consent to Research

    a. Psychologists use language that is reasonably understandable to research participants in obtaining their informed consent (except as provided in Standard 6.12, Dispensing With Informed Consent). Such informed consent is appropriately documented.

b. Using language that is reasonably understandable to participants, psychologists inform participants of the nature of the research; they inform participants that they are free to participate or to decline to participate or to withdraw from the research; they explain the foreseeable consequences of declining or withdrawing; they inform participants of significant factors that may be expected to influence their willingness to participate (such as risks, discomfort, adverse effects, or limitations on confidentiality, except as provided in Standard 6.15, Deception in Research); and they explain other aspects about which the prospective participants inquire.

c. When psychologists conduct research with individuals such as students or subordinates, psychologists take special care to protect the prospective participants from adverse consequences of declining or withdrawing from participation.

d. When research participation is a course requirement or opportunity for extra credit, the prospective participant is given the choice of equitable alternative activities.

e. For persons who are legally incapable of giving informed consent, psychologists nevertheless 1) provide an appropriate explanation, 2) obtain the participant's assent, and 3) obtain appropriate permission from a legally authorized person, if such substitute consent is permitted by law.

6.12 Dispensing With Informed Consent

Before determining that planned research (such as research involving only anonymous questionnaires, naturalistic observations, or certain kinds of archival research) does not require the informed consent of research participants, psychologists consider applicable regulations and institutional review board requirements, and they consult with colleagues as appropriate.

6.13 Informed Consent in Research Filming or Recording

Psychologists obtain informed consent from research participants prior to filming or recording them in any form, unless the research involves simply naturalistic observations in public places and it is not anticipated that the recording will be used in a manner that could cause personal identification or harm.

6.14 Offering Inducements for Research Participants

a. In offering professional services as an inducement to obtain research participants, psychologists make clear the nature of the services, as well as the risks, obligations, and limitations. (See also Standard 1.18, Barter [With Patients or Clients].)

b. Psychologists do not offer excessive or inappropriate financial or other inducements to obtain research participants, particularly when it might tend to coerce participation.

6.15 Deception in Research

a. Psychologists do not conduct a study involving deception unless they have determined that the use of deceptive techniques is justified by the study's prospective scientific, educational, or applied value and that equally effective alternative procedures that do not use deception are not feasible.

b. Psychologists never deceive research participants about significant aspects that would affect their willingness to participate, such as physical risks, discomfort, or unpleasant emotional experiences.

c. Any other deception that is an integral feature of the design and conduct of an experiment must be explained to participants as early as is feasible, preferably at the conclusion of their participation, but no later than at the conclusion of the research. (See also Standard 6.18, Providing Participants With Information About the Study.)

6.16 Sharing and Utilizing Data

Psychologists inform research participants of their anticipated sharing or further use of personally identifiable research data and of the possibility of unanticipated future uses.

6.17 Minimizing Invasiveness

In conducting research, psychologists interfere with the participants or milieu from which data are collected only in a manner that is warranted by an appropriate research design and that is consistent with psychologists' roles as scientific investigators.

6.18 Providing Participants With Information About the Study

 a. Psychologists provide a prompt opportunity for participants to obtain appropriate information about the nature, results, and conclusions of the research, and psychologists attempt to correct any misconceptions that participants may have.
 b. If scientific or humane values justify delaying or withholding this information, psychologists take reasonable measures to reduce the risk of harm.

6.19 Honoring Commitments

Psychologists take reasonable measures to honor all commitments they have made to research participants.

Canadian Psychological Association (CPA)*

 II. 22 Debrief research participants in such a way that the participants' knowledge is enhanced and the participants have a sense of contribution to knowledge.
 II. 39 Debrief research participants in such a way that any harm caused can be discerned, and act to correct any resultant harm.

Avoidance of Deception

 III. 23 Not engage in deception in any service activity.
 III. 24 Not engage in deception in research or the use of techniques which might be interpreted as deception, in research or service activities, if there are alternative procedures available and/or if the negative effects cannot be predicted or offset.
 III. 25 Not engage in deception in research or the use of techniques which might be interpreted as deception in research or service activities, if it would interfere with the individual's understanding of facts which clearly might influence a decision to give informed consent.

---

*Copyright 1993. Canadian Psychological Association. Reprinted with permission.

III. 26 Use the minimum necessary deception in research or techniques which might be interpreted as deception in research, or service activities.

III. 27 Provide research participants, during debriefing, with a clarification of the nature of the study, if deception or the use of techniques which could be interpreted as deception has occurred. In such circumstances, psychologists would seek to remove any misconceptions which might have arisen and to reestablish any trust which might have been lost, assuring the participant during debriefing that the real or apparent deception was neither arbitrary nor capricious.

III. 28 Act to reestablish with clients any trust which might have been lost due to the use of techniques which might be interpreted as deception.

III. 29 Seek an independent and adequate ethical review of the risks to public or individual trust and of safeguards to protect such trust for any research which uses deception or techniques which might be interpreted as deception, before making a decision to proceed.

How to Read Research Articles

You may never conduct a scientific experiment. Nevertheless, the results of scientific experiments will have an impact on your life. You may not read scientific journals but you will see media reports of scientific discoveries. In this sense, you will be a consumer of research. We hope that after reading this book you will be a more critical consumer of research.

For instance, most people are aware of the impact of cholesterol on heart disease. Indeed, people have changed their diet after reading about research. They made the decision to change based on media reports rather than on actual research reports. Most popular media reports of scientific discoveries do not present enough information for readers to make up their minds about the validity of the research. After reading this book you know many of the things that can go wrong with research. Knowing these things, you should be sceptical of breakthroughs reported in the media.

Similarly, when you read a journal article reporting research, you should read it with a sceptical, probing, mind-set. You should be seeking flaws in the design. The following is an outline of questions designed to point to potential areas of weakness on which to focus as you read research reports.

I. Introduction
   A. Why was the research done? What are the researchers trying to test?
   B. What is the link between the theory (or applied problem) and the research hypothesis? Are the researchers testing what they think they're testing?
   C. Is the literature review adequate?
II. Introduction or method section
   A. What was the research hypothesis?
   B. What was the null hypothesis?
III. Method section
   A. What were the independent variables?
   B. What were the dependent variables?
   C. What are the threats, if any,
      1. to internal validity?
      2. to construct validity? Do the operational variables in this section correspond to the conceptual variables in the introduction?
IV. Results
   A. Presentation
      1. Are descriptive statistics presented, e.g., means and standard deviations?
      2. Are the tables easily understood?
      3. Is there information not included that you would like to see included?
      4. Is there unnecessary information?
   B. How were the data analyzed?
   C. Were the analyses appropriate?
V. Discussion
   A. Do the authors
      1. interpret the results appropriately?
      2. relate the results to the introduction?
      3. discuss all of the potential problems with their results?
   B. What are the threats to the external validity of the results?
VI. Design—if you could redesign this study, how would you do it? (This is a good way to discover some of the flaws in the research reported.)

GLOSSARY

Absolute measure (of a population)
Description of means or percentages in a population. For instance, 73 percent of people in this population are satisfied with their economic condition. Cf., Relative measure (of a population).

Accidental sample Nonprobability sample in which the researcher selects the first set of elements encountered.

Behavior (survey questions about) Questions about actions a person took or plans to take. Example: "Did you take a vacation in 1993?"

Biased sample Sample with characteristics that do not resemble those of all of the people who could have been sampled.

Captive audience Subjects in a study who do not choose to be present and who are not free to leave.

Case study Study carried out on one person or case, usually descriptive in nature.

Causal hypotheses Possible explanations for an observed relationship between two variables. Usually stated as "If X then Y."

Check on manipulation Measures (in an experiment) to assess the effectiveness of the manipulation of the independent variable.

Closed-ended questions Questions where respondents must select a response from the set of alternatives presented.

Commons dilemma Mixed-motive situation in which a group of people try to manage a scarce but renewable resource (or when the people must decide whether or not to contribute to some common resource).

Complex questions (in survey) Questions that contain difficult words, negatives, and double negatives that may confuse respondents and contribute to random error. Example: "Teaching assistants should not be allowed to grade nonobjective examinations."

Computer simulation Computer program designed to "behave" like research subjects. Used to derive and test hypotheses.

Conceptual replication A study, similar to an earlier one, but with different operationalizations of the critical variables.

Conceptual validity Extent to which a researcher can generalize from the operational variable to the conceptual variable.

Conceptual variables Theoretical variables that cannot be directly manipulated in an experiment.

Concomitant variation Two variables change together. This can be positive (as one increases the other increases) or negative (as one increases the other decreases). Also referred to as correlation.

Concurrent validity A type of criterion-oriented validity established by correlating a measuring instrument with another one with known validity.

Confidence interval An interval drawn around a sample mean that has a specified probability of including the population mean.

Construct validity Validity that is established by comparing the scores obtained with a measuring instrument with theoretically expected values.

Context bias See Interviewer bias.

Control group Subjects in an experiment who are treated identically to those in the experimental group except that they are not exposed to the experimental treatment.

Correlational designs Nonexperimental designs in which variables are measured but not manipulated or controlled.

Criterion-oriented validity Validity that is established by correlating scores obtained with a measuring instrument with an outside criterion that is generally accepted as valid.

Cronbach's alpha Measure of test reliability based on intercorrelations among the test items.

Debriefing Explaining the research purposes and procedures to participants after the data have been obtained. Participants' perceptions and suggestions may also be elicited.

Demand characteristics Cues (other than those conveyed by the experimenter) that let the subject know what behaviors the researcher expects.

Demographic survey questions Questions about topics such as age, sex, marital status, employment status, and occupation.

Dependent variable Variable observed or measured by researcher. In causal hypothesis, "If X then Y," Y is the dependent variable.

Double-barrelled survey questions Statements with which respondents are asked to agree or disagree but that contain more than one complete thought. Contribute to random error. Example: "University admission standards should be raised to reduce overcrowding."

Double-blind procedure A procedure used in experiments in which neither the subject nor the experimenter is aware of the experimental condition to which the subject has been assigned.

Element A single unit of the population to be sampled.

Experimental group Subjects in an experiment who are exposed to the experimental treatment.

Experimental realism When subjects believe that what is happening in the experiment is real, worth attending to, and influenced by their own actions.

Experimenter bias A type of systematic bias inadvertently introduced by the behavior of the experimenter.

External validity Ability to generalize research results. A study has external validity if its results apply to populations and settings other than those actually studied.

Face-to-face surveys Surveys in which interviewers establish direct personal contact with the respondents.

Face validity Apparent similarity between the conceptual variables and the operational ones.

Fail-safe number The number of nonsignificant outcomes needed before a meta-analyst's conclusion about a significant effect would be invalidated.

File-drawer problem Problem in meta-analysis. For every study with significant results that appears in the journals, there may be countless other "failures" in researchers' file drawers.

Game playing An alternative to deception used most extensively in studies of bargaining and decision making.

Generalization (absolute) Inference about population percentages or means based on sample characteristics. Example: If 73 percent of the people in a sample are satisfied with their economic condition, then 73 percent of the people in the population should also be satisfied.

Generalization (relative) Inference that some group in the population is more likely than another to hold a particular attitude, opinion, belief, etc. Example: If in a sample, children are more likely than adults to believe in ghosts, then in the population, children should be more likely to believe in ghosts.

Hawthorne effect Changes in the behavior of research participants caused by their knowledge that they are part of a study.

History (threat of) What appears to be the effect of an independent variable is the effect of the passage of time or events occurring outside of the experiment.

Independent variable The causal variable. The variable manipulated by the researcher in an experiment. In causal hypothesis, "If X then Y," X is the independent variable.

Instrumentation (threat of) What appears to be the effect of an independent variable is the effect of a change in measuring instruments.

Interaction In multi-factor designs, the effect of one independent variable depends on the level of another.

Internal reliability See Intra-test reliability.

Internal validity The effectiveness of a research design in minimizing alternative explanations for obtained results.

Inter-rater reliability Reliability of a measuring instrument established by correlating the ratings of two (or more) judges.

Inter-test reliability Reliability of a test established by correlating scores obtained by respondents at two separate times. Also known as test–retest reliability.

Interviewer (context) bias Systematic bias introduced by the characteristics or the behavior of the person asking the questions.

Intra-test reliability Reliability of a test established by correlating subjects' responses to separate items on the same test. Known also as internal reliability.

Mail survey Survey questionnaires are mailed to respondents and returned by mail.

Main effect In multi-factor designs, the effect of each of the independent variables considered separately.

Maturation (threat of) What appears to be the effect of an independent variable is the effect of changes or events within the people being observed.

Meta-analysis Procedures for comparing, combining, and drawing conclusions from the results of several independent studies.

Mixed-motive game A situation in which there are pressures on people both to compete and to cooperate.

Mortality (threat of) What appears to be the effect of the independent variable is the effect of people dropping out of the experiment before it is finished.

Multi-factor designs Experimental designs in which two or more variables are manipulated.

Multi-stage random sampling Selection of a sample of respondents using random sampling at successive stages, e.g., randomly selecting states, then cities, then streets, and then houses.

Mundane realism The extent to which an experimental situation resembles the world outside the laboratory.

N Abbreviation for "Number". The number of independent units, usually subjects, being studied.

Nonattitudes (problem of) Respondent has no attitude on issues being studied. Responses simply may contribute to random error.

Nonmonotonic survey questions Questions that can be answered in the same way for different reasons. Example: "Only material showing nudity and violence should be censored."

Nonprobability (or nonrandom) sample A sampling procedure that makes it impossible to estimate the likelihood that any element will be included in the sample.

Nonrandom sample See Nonprobability sample.

Nonreactive measures See Unobtrusive measures.

Observed score Score obtained as a result of a measuring process. The observed score reflects, in varying degrees, the true score, systematic bias, and random error.

Obtrusive (reactive) measures A measurement procedure that makes people aware that some aspect of their behavior is being studied and recorded.

Open-ended questions Questions that allow respondents to answer in their own words.

Operational variables Variables in which the methods of measurement and manipulation have been specified.

Over-represented (in sample) The percentage of elements in a sample exceeds the percentage of these elements in the population. Example: A sample of U.S. citizens in which 75 percent of the persons are female.

Pilot study Study conducted before the main project to assess the feasibility of procedures, etc.

Predictive validity A type of criterion-oriented validity in which the ability of a measuring instrument to predict future behavior is assessed.

Prisoner's dilemma A mixed-motive situation used to investigate decision making in conflict situations.

Probability (or random) sample A sample in which all elements of a population have a specifiable probability (usually an equal probability) of being included.

Psychological state (survey questions about) Questions about a person's perceptions, attitudes, opinions, feelings, etc. Example: "Do you think that Thomas Jefferson was a good president?"

Purposive sample Nonprobability sample in which the researcher selects the most interesting or informative elements of the population.

Quasi-control Method of assessing the impact of demand characteristics in an experiment.

Quasi-experimental design Nonexperimental designs to study the impact of an independent variable when people have not been randomly assigned to conditions. Control groups are used to eliminate alternative explanations for results.

Questionnaire Measuring instrument commonly used to collect information in an experiment or a survey.

Random assignment A method of assigning subjects to experimental conditions using random numbers drawn from a table or generated by a computer.

Random error Variability in a dependent measure produced by factors that the researcher does not or cannot control, e.g., time of day.

Random sample See Probability sample.

Reactive intervention Policy implemented in reaction to an extreme condition. Can be a threat to the internal validity of a study to evaluate that policy.

Reactive measures See Obtrusive measures.

Reactivity (threat of) Threat to external validity caused by subjects' awareness that they are being studied.

Relative measure (of a population) Comparison of group means, attitudes, etc. within a population. Example: "Children are more likely to believe in ghosts than are adults." Cf., Absolute measure (of a population).

Reliability Repeatability of measure. Indicates the relative absence of random error in the measurement of a dependent variable.

Representative sample A sample in which the distribution of element characteristics resembles that in the population from which it is drawn.

Response rate The number of respondents completing a survey expressed as a proportion of the total number contacted.

Role playing An alternative to experimental procedures that involves deceiving subjects. Subjects are asked to behave the way a person in some particular situation would behave.

Sampling frame Complete list of elements in the population to be sampled.

Selectivity (threat of) The possibility that subjects were selected for experimental conditions in some biased fashion, either by themselves or by the experimenter.

Simple random sample A sample obtained from a complete list of elements in the population by using random numbers from a table or a computer program.

Single-factor design Experimental designs in which only one variable is manipulated.

Small-N designs Nonexperimental designs to study the impact of an independent variable when there are few subjects.

Social desirability bias Systematic bias created by research participants' desire to present a favorable image of themselves.

Stratified random sample A procedure in which the researcher divides the population into subgroups or "strata" and then draws a random sample from each of the subgroups. Example: Random samples of people under 20 years old, between 21 and 40, between 41 and 60, etc.

Systematic bias Distortion in a dependent measure produced by a factor that exerts a consistent influence (either upward or downward) on each score in a set.

Telephone survey Survey in which questions are asked by an interviewer over the telephone.

Test–retest reliability See Inter-test reliability.

Test validity The extent to which a test accurately measures what it is supposed to measure.

Testing (threat of) What appears to be the effect of an independent variable is the effect of the measurement and testing process itself.

Under-represented (in sample)
The percentage of elements in a sample is less than the percentage of these elements in the population. Example: A sample of U.S. citizens in which 25 percent of the persons are female.

Unobtrusive (nonreactive) measures
A measurement procedure in which people are not aware that some aspect of their behavior is being studied and recorded.

Validity Accuracy of a measuring instrument. Is the instrument measuring what it is supposed to be measuring?

Wording bias Systematic bias in responses introduced by the way a question is worded.

REFERENCES

Abelson, R. P. (1968). Simulation of social behavior. In G. Lindzey & E. Aronson (Eds.), *Handbook of social psychology* (2nd ed., Vol. 2., pp. 274–356). Reading, MA: Addison-Wesley.

Adair, J. G., Dushenko, T. W., & Lindsay, R. C. (1985). Ethical regulations and their impact on research practice. *American Psychologist, 40,* 59–72.

Allison, S. T., & Messick, D. M. (1985). The group attribution error. *Journal of Experimental Social Psychology, 21,* 563–579.

Amato, P. R., & Keith, B. (1991). Parental divorce and the well-being of children: A meta-analysis. *Psychological Bulletin, 110,* 26–46.

Aronson, E., Ellsworth, P. C., Carlsmith, J. M., & Gonzales, J. H. (1990). *Methods of research in social psychology* (2nd ed.). New York: McGraw-Hill.

Aronson, E., & Mills, J. (1959). The effect of severity of initiation on liking for a group. *Journal of Abnormal and Social Psychology, 59,* 177–181.

Bangert-Drowns, R. L. (1986). Review of developments in meta-analytic method. *Psychological Bulletin, 99,* 388–399.

Barton, A. J. (1958). Asking the embarrassing question. *Public Opinion Quarterly, 22,* 67–68.

Baumrind, D. (1985). Research using intentional deception: Ethical issues revisited. *American Psychologist, 40,* 165–174.

Bochner, S. (1971). The use of unobtrusive measures in cross-cultural attitudes research. In R. M. Berndt (Ed.), *A question of choice: An Australian aboriginal dilemma.* Nedlands, W.A.: University of Western Australia Press.

Braver, M. C., & Braver, S .L. (1988). Statistical treatment of the Solomon Four-Group Design: A meta-analytic approach. *Psychological Bulletin, 104,* 150–154.

Breast Implant Survey Considered Dismal Failure. (1992, August 11). *The St. John's [Newfoundland] Evening Telegram,* p. 16. From Vancouver, Canadian Press.

175

Brewer, M. B., & Kramer, R. M. (1986). Choice behavior in social dilemmas: Effects of social identity, group size, and decision framing. *Journal of Personality and Social Psychology, 50,* 543–549.

Brigham, J. C., & Cook, S. W. (1969). The influence of attitude on the recall of controversial material: A failure to confirm. *Journal of Experimental Social Psychology, 5,* 240–243.

Campbell, D. T., & Stanley, J. C. (1963). *Experimental and quasi-experimental designs for research.* Skokie, IL: Rand McNally.

Carlsmith, J. M., Ellsworth, P. C., & Aronson, E. (1976). *Methods of research in social psychology.* Reading, MA: Addison-Wesley.

Carmines, E. G., & Zeller, R. A. (1979). Reliability and validity assessment. In J. Sullivan (Ed.), *Quantitative applications in the social sciences.* Newbury Park, CA: Sage Publications.

Christensen, L. (1988). Deception in psychological research: When is its use justified? *Personality and Social Psychology Bulletin, 14,* 664–675.

Cohen, J. (1988). *Statistical power analysis in the behavioral sciences.* Hillsdale, NJ: Erlbaum.

Cohn, L. D. (1991). Sex differences in the course of personality development: A meta-analysis. *Psychological Bulletin, 109,* 252–266.

Connidis, I. (1983). Living arrangement choices of older residents: Assessing quantitative results with qualitative data. *Canadian Journal of Sociology, 8,* 359–375.

Cook, T. D., & Campbell, D. T. (1979). *Quasi-experimentation: Design and analysis issues for field settings.* Skokie, IL: Rand McNally.

Cronbach, L. J., & Meehl, P. E. (1955). Construct validity in psychological tests. *Psychological Bulletin, 52,* 281–302.

Darroch, R. K., & Steiner, I. D. (1970). Role playing: An alternative to laboratory research? *Journal of Personality, 38,* 302–311.

Deutsch, M., & Krauss, R. M. (1962). The effect of threat upon interpersonal bargaining. *Journal of Abnormal and Social Psychology, 61,* 181–189.

Doob, A. N., & Macdonald, G. E. (1979). Television viewing and fear of victimization: Is the relationship causal? *Journal of Personality and Social Psychology, 37,* 170–179.

Durlak, J. A., Fuhrman, T., & Lampman, C. (1991). Effectiveness of cognitive-behavior therapy for maladapting children: A meta-analysis. *Psychological Bulletin, 110,* 204–214.

Eagly, A. H., & Johnson, B. T. (1990). Gender and leadership style: A meta-analysis. *Psychological Bulletin, 108,* 233–256.

Eagly, A. H., Makhijani, M. G., & Klonsky, B. G. (1992). Gender and the evaluation of leaders: A meta-analysis. *Psychological Bulletin, 111,* 3–22.

Ebbesen, E. B., & Konecni, V. J. (1975, September). *Analysis of legal decision-making: Bail setting and sentencing.* Paper presented to meeting of American Psychological Association, Chicago.

Eron, L. D., Huesmann, L. R., Lefkowitz, M. M., & Walder, L. O. (1972). Does television violence cause aggression? *American Psychologist, 27,* 253–263.

Festinger, L., Riecken, H., & Schachter, S. (1956). *When prophecy fails.* MN: University of Minnesota Press.

Freedman, J. L. (1969). Role-playing: Psychology by consensus. *Journal of Personality and Social Psychology, 13,* 107–114.

Gallo, P. S. (1966). Effects of increased incentives upon the use of threat in bargaining. *Journal of Personality and Social Psychology, 4,* 14–20.

Gantner, A. B., & Taylor, S. P. (1988). Human physical aggression as a function of diazepam. *Personality and Social Psychology Bulletin, 14,* 479–484.

Gerbner, G., Gross, L., Eleey, M. F., Fox, S., Jackson-Beeck, M., & Signorielli, N. (1976). *Trends in network television drama and viewer conceptions of social reality, 1967–1975. Violence profile number 7.* Philadelphia, PA.: The Annenberg School of Communications, University of Pennsylvania.

Gergen, K. J. (1973). Social psychology as history. *Journal of Personality and Social Psychology, 26,* 309–320.

Greenberg, M. S. (1967). Role-playing: An alternative to deception. *Journal of Personality and Social Psychology, 7,* 152–157.

Greenwald, A. G., & Sakumura, J. S. (1967). Attitude and selective learning: Where are the phenomena of yesteryear? *Journal of Experimental Social Psychology, 7,* 387–399.

Harris, L. & Associates (1975). *The myth and reality of aging in America.* Washington, DC: The National Council on the Aging.

Hastie, R. (1988). A computer simulation model of person memory. *Journal of Experimental Social Psychology, 24,* 423–447.

Hays, W. L., & Winkler, R. L. (1970). *Statistics: Probability, inference, and Decision* (Vol. 1). New York: Holt, Rinehart & Winston.

Hedges, B. (1990). Designing Samples. Report of the ESCR Survey Methods Seminar. *Joint Centre for Survey Methods Newsletter, 11,* 1.

Hedges, L. V., & Olkin, I. (1985). *Statistical methods for meta-analysis.* Orlando, FL: Academic Press.

Heider, F. (1958). *The psychology of interpersonal relations.* New York: John Wiley.

Higbee, K. L., & Wells, M. G. (1972). Some research trends in social psychology during the 1960s. *American Psychologist, 27,* 963–966.

Hofling, C. K., Brotzman, E., Dalrymple, S., Graves, N., & Pierce, C. M. (1966). An experimental study in nurse-physician relationships. *Journal of Nervous and Mental Disease, 143,* 171–180.

Holmes, D. S., & Bennett, D. H. (1974). Experiments to answer questions raised by the use of deception in psychological research. *Journal of Personality and Social Psychology, 29,* 358–367.

Homans, G. C. (1965). Group factors in worker productivity. In H. Proshansky, & B. Seidenberg (Eds.), *Basic studies in social psychology.* New York: Holt, Rinehart & Winston.

Horowitz, I. A., & Rothschild, B. H. (1970). Conformity as a function of deception and role-playing. *Journal of Personality and Social Psychology, 14,* 224–226.

Hovland, C. I. (1959). Reconciling conflicting results derived from experimental and survey studies of attitude change. *American Psychologist, 14,* 8–17.

Hovland, C. I., Lumsdaine, A. A., & Sheffield, F. D. (1965). *Studies in social psychology in World War II* (Vol. 3). Experiments on mass communication. New York: John Wiley. (Original work published 1949, Princeton University Press).

Hunter, J. E., & Schmidt, F. L. (1990). *Methods of meta-analysis: Correcting error and bias in research findings.* Newbury Park, CA: Sage Publications.

Hyde, J. S., Fennema, E., & Lamon, S. J. (1990). Gender differences in mathematics performance: A meta-analysis. *Psychological Bulletin, 107,* 139–155.

Jorgenson, D. O., & Papciak, A. S. (1981). The effects of communication, resource feedback, and identifiability on behavior in a simulated commons. *Journal of Experimental Social Psychology, 17,* 373–385.

Judd, C. M., Smith, E. R., & Kidder, L. H. (1991). *Research methods in social relations* (6th ed.). Fort Worth: Holt, Rinehart & Winston.

Kelman, H. C. (1967). Human use of human subjects: The problem of deception in social psychological experiments. *Psychological Bulletin, 67,* 1–11.

Kramer, R. M., & Brewer, M. B. (1984). Effects of group identity on resource use in a simulated commons dilemma. *Journal of Personality and Social Psychology, 46,* 1044–1057.

Kratochwill, T. R. (1978). *Single subject research. Strategies for evaluating change.* New York: Academic Press.

Kruglanski, A. W. (1973). Much ado about the "volunteer-artifacts." *Journal of Personality and Social Psychology, 28,* 348–354.

Levine, J. M., & Murphy, G. (1943). The learning and forgetting of controversial material. *Journal of Abnormal and Social Psychology, 38,* 507–517.

Lindzey, G., & Aronson, E. (1985). *The handbook of social psychology.* (3rd ed.) New York: Random House.

Lord, C. G., Lepper, M. R., & Preston, E. (1984). Considering the opposite: A corrective strategy for social judgment. *Journal of Personality and Social Psychology, 47,* 1231–1243.

Lytton, H., & Romney, D. M. (1991). Parents' differential socialization of boys and girls: A meta-analysis. *Psychological Bulletin, 109,* 267–296.

Mahoney, M. J. (1977). Publication prejudices: An experimental study of confirmatory bias in the peer review system. *Cognitive Therapy and Research, 1,* 161–175.

Mathieu, J. E., & Zajac, D. M. (1990). A review and meta-analysis of the antecedents, correlates, and consequences of organizational commitment. *Psychological Bulletin, 108,* 171–194.

McGuire, W. J. (1967). Some impending reorientations in social psychology. *Journal of Experimental Social Psychology, 3,* 124–139.

Means, B., Nigam, A., Zarrow, M., Loftus, E., & Donaldson, M. S. (1989). *Autobiographical memory for health-related events*. National Center for Health Statistics. Hyattsville, MD: Vital and Health Statistics 6(2).

Milgram, S. (1963). Behavioral study of obedience. *Journal of Abnormal and Social Psychology, 67,* 371–378.

Miller, A. G. (1972). Role-playing: An alternative to deception? *American Psychologist, 27,* 623–636.

Mother Jones Magazine (1986, November). Foundation for National Progress, p. 10.

Newcomb, T. M. (1961). *The acquaintance process*. New York: Holt, Rinehart & Winston.

Nowak, A., Szamrej, J. M., & Latané, B. (1990). From private attitude to public opinion: A dynamic theory of social impact. *Psychological Review, 97,* 362–376.

Oakes, W. (1972). External validity and the use of real people as subjects. *American Psychologist, 27,* 959–962.

Okun, M. A., Olding, R. W., & Cohn, C. M. G. (1990). A meta-analysis of subjective well-being interventions among elders. *Psychological Bulletin, 108,* 257–266.

Orne, M. T. (1962). On the social psychology of the psychological experiment: With particular reference to demand characteristics and their implications. *American Psychologist, 17,* 776–783.

Orne, M. T., & Evans, F. (1965). Social control in the psychological experiment: Antisocial behavior and hypnosis. *Journal of Personality and Social Psychology, 1,* 189–200.

Orne, M. T., & Scheibe, K. E. (1964). The contribution of nondeprivation factors in the production of sensory deprivation effects: The psychology of the "panic button." *Journal of Abnormal and Social Psychology, 68,* 3–12.

Ostrom, T. M. (1988). Computer simulation: The third symbol system. *Journal of Experimental Social Psychology, 24,* 381–392.

Pleasant smell. (1992, 1 October). *The St. John's [Newfoundland] Evening Telegram*. From Las Vegas, Associated Press.

Rea, L. M., & Parker, R. A. (1992). *Designing and conducting survey research*. San Francisco: Jossey–Bass.

Recession-Induced Funk Hitting Canadians Hard. (1992, 1 October). *The St. John's [Newfoundland] Evening Telegram,* p. 1. From Toronto, Canadian Press.

Reis, H. T., & Stiller, J. (1992). Publication trends in JPSP: A three decade review. *Personality and Social Psychology Bulletin, 18,* 465–472.

Ring, K. (1967). Experimental social psychology: Some sober questions about some frivolous values. *Journal of Experimental Social Psychology, 3,* 113–123.

Roberts, J. V. (1985). The attitude-memory relationship after 40 years: A meta-analysis of the literature. *Basic and Applied Social Psychology, 6,* 221–241.

Robinson, J. P., Shaver, P. R., & Wrightsman, L. S. (Eds.), (1991). *Measures of personality and social psychological attitudes.* San Diego, CA: Academic Press.

Rosenberg, M. J., & Abelson, R. P. (1960). An analysis of cognitive balancing. In M. J. Rosenberg, C. I. Hovland, W. J. McGuire, R. P. Abelson, & J. W. Brehm (Eds.), *Attitude organization and change: An analysis of consistency among attitude components.* (pp. 112–163). New Haven, CT: Yale University Press.

Rosenthal, R. (1963). On the social psychology of the psychological experiment: The experimenter's hypothesis as unintended determinant of experimental results. *American Scientist, 51,* 268–283.

Rosenthal, R. (1979). The "file drawer problem" and tolerance for null results. *Psychological Bulletin, 86,* 638–641.

Rosenthal, R. (1984). *Meta-analytic procedures for social research.* Newbury Park, CA: Sage Publications.

Rosenthal, R., & Fode, K. L. (1963a). The effect of experimenter bias on the performance of the albino rat. *Behavioral Science, 8,* 183–189.

Rosenthal, R., & Fode, K. L. (1963b). Three experiments in experimenter bias. *Psychological Reports, 12,* 491–511.

Rosenthal, R., & Rosnow, R.L. (1969). *Artifact in behavioral research.* New York: Academic Press.

Ross, A. S., & Grant, M. J. (1982). An evaluation of the St. John's unified family court pilot project. Unpublished report to the Department[s] of Justice [Newfoundland and Canada].

Ross, A. S., & White, S. (1987). Shoplifting, impaired driving and refusing the breathalyser: On seeing one's name in a public place. *Evaluation Review, 11,* 254–260.

Rowell, J. A., & Dawson, C. J. (1981). Volume, conservation and instruction: A classroom based Solomon-Four Group study of conflict. *Journal of Research in Science Teaching, 18,* 533–546.

Rowland, L. W. (1939). Will hypnotized persons try to harm themselves or others? *Journal of Abnormal and Social Psychology, 34,* 114–117.

Rubenstein, C., Shaver, P., & Peplau, L. A. (1979). Loneliness. *Human Nature, 2,* 59–65.

Sarnoff, I., & Zimbardo, P. (1961). Anxiety, fear and social affiliation. *Journal of Abnormal and Social Psychology, 62,* 356–363.

Sato, K. (1987). Distribution of the cost of maintaining common resources. *Journal of Experimental Social Psychology, 23,* 19–31.

Schachter, S. (1959). *The psychology of affiliation: Experimental studies of the sources of gregariousness.* Stanford, CA: Stanford University Press.

Schmitt, B. H., Gilovich, T., Goore, N., & Joseph, L. (1986). Mere presence and social facilitation: One more time. *Journal of Experimental Social Psychology, 22,* 242–248.

Schroeder, D. A., Jensen, T. D., Reed, A. J., Sullivan, D. K., & Schwab, M. (1983). The actions of others as determinants of behavior in social trap situations. *Journal of Experimental Social Psychology, 19,* 522–539.

Schultz, D. P. (1969). The human subject in psychological research. *Psychological Bulletin, 72,* 214–228.

Schwartz, N., & Bless, H. (1992). Scandals and the public's trust in politicians: Assimilation and contrast effects. *Personality and Social Psychology Bulletin, 18,* 574–579.

Sharpe, D., Adair, J. G., & Roese, N. J. (1992). Twenty years of deception research: A decline in subjects' trust? *Personality and Social Psychology Bulletin, 18,* 585–590.

Sigall, H., Aronson, E., & Van Hoose, T. (1970). The cooperative subject: Myth or reality? *Journal of Experimental Social Psychology, 6,* 1–10.

Social Science Research Council. (1975). *Basic background items for U.S. household surveys.* Washington, DC: Center for Coordination of Research on Social Indicators, Social Science Research Council.

Spangler, W. D. (1992). Validity of questionnaire and TAT measures of need for achievement: Two meta-analyses. *Psychological Bulletin, 112,* 140–154.

Stasser, G. (1988). Computer simulation as a research tool: The DISCUSS model of group decision making. *Journal of Experimental Social Psychology, 24,* 393–422.

Statistics Canada (1980). *Social Concepts Directory: A Guide Toward Standardization in Statistical Surveys.* Ottawa, Ontario: Statistics Canada, 12–560.

Walster, E., Berscheid, E., Abrahams, D., & Aronson, E. (1967). Effectiveness of de-briefing following deception experiments. *Journal of Personality and Social Psychology, 4,* 371–380.

Waly, P., & Cook, S. W. (1966). Attitude as a determinant of learning and memory: A failure to confirm. *Journal of Personality and Social Psychology, 4,* 280–288.

Webb, E. J., Campbell, D. T., Schwartz, D., & Sechrest, L. (1966). *Unobtrusive measures: Nonreactive research in the social sciences.* Skokie, IL: Rand McNally.

West, S. G., Newsom, J. T., & Fenaughty, A. M. (1992). Publication trends in JPSP: Stability and change in topics, methods, and theories across two decades. *Personality and Social Psychology Bulletin, 18,* 473–484.

Whyte, W. F. (1943). *Street corner society.* Chicago: University of Chicago Press.

Willis, R. H., & Willis, Y. A. (1970). Role playing versus deception: An experimental comparison. *Journal of Personality and Social Psychology, 16,* 472–477.

Wolf, T. M., Kissling, G. E., & Burgess, L. A. (1986). Lifestyle characteristics during medical school: A four-year cross-sectional study. *Psychological Reports, 39,* 179–189.

Young, P. C. (1952). Antisocial uses of hypnosis. In L.M. Le Cron (Ed.), *Experimental hypnosis.* New York: Macmillan.

INDEX